A Taste of Well-Being

Sadhguru's insights for your gastronomics

ISHA YOGA CENTRE

HarperCollins *Publishers* India

First published in India in 2016 by Harper Element
An imprint of HarperCollins *Publishers* India
4th Floor, Tower A, Building No. 10, Phase II, DLF Cyber City,
Gurugram, Haryrna - 122002
www.harpercollins.co.in

This edition published in India by HarperCollins *Publishers* in 2019

28

P-ISBN: 978-93-5136-378-1
E-ISBN: 978-93-5136-379-8

Typeset in 11.5/14 Arapey
Jojy Philip New Delhi 110 015

Printed and bound at
Thomson Press (India) Ltd

Contents

Contents

vi

Contents

Contents

Contents

The True Joy of Eating

Sadhguru

Food is life giving away its own life to make your life. If only you were aware that so many lives are giving up their own lives to sustain your own, you would eat with enormous gratitude. If you eat with that kind of gratitude, you will naturally eat only to the extent that it is necessary. The food will behave in a completely different way in your system; the way you treat it is the way it treats you.

Your consciousness is very important in determining how a certain food behaves in your system. Let us say two people are eating food with exactly the same levels of nourishment and their health and absorption rates are about equal. One person eats the food with joy while the other simply eats it as nourishment. The one who eats with joy will need much less food and will get better nourishment than the other person. There is scientific evidence to prove this. Every human being who is a little sensitive to life always knows this. If you eat with gratitude and reverence, you will see whatever you eat will work wonderfully for you.

The true joy of eating is that you are conscious of some other life willing to become a part of you, to merge and mingle with your own life and become you. This is the greatest pleasure a human being knows – in some way something that is not him is willing to become a part of him. This is what you call love. This is what people call devotion. This is the ultimate goal of the spiritual process. Whether it is lust, passion, devotion or the ultimate enlightenment, it is all the same – it is just the scale. If it happens between two people we call it passion; if it happens with a larger group we call it love; if it happens much more indiscriminately we call it compassion; if it happens without even a form around you, it is called devotion; if it happens in its ultimate scale, we call it Enlightenment.

This beautiful process of constant demonstration of the oneness of existence is happening at your mealtime every day. Food, eating, is a demonstration of the oneness of existence. Something that was a plant, something that was a seed, something that was an animal or a fish or a bird, just merging and becoming a human being, is clear demonstration of the oneness of existence, of the hand of the Creator in everything that is. Make the simple act of eating into fulfilling the will of Creation and the tremendous experience of knowing the joy of Union.

A Taste of Isha

Just a few decades ago, the way humans looked at food was largely influenced by local culture, tradition and seasons. Local produce, fast becoming a rare and expensive commodity, was once the natural diet of millions. What is now referred to as the 'slow food movement' was just the way of the world. But now that we have moved into an era when everything under the sun is accessible to us, one would think that we would be better equipped to understand what we should or should not eat. Unfortunately, that is not the case. The truth is, with the steady stream of half-baked research coming our way through online and print media, we have regressed to a state of confusion. Food products labelled 'healthy' one day are abruptly dismissed as 'lethal' the very next. Foods touted as nutritious and life-enhancing by one study are declared carcinogenic by another. The latest 'celebrity diet' is always around the corner, waiting to be trashed by nutritionists. So taking all this into consideration, what is the correct, balanced diet for our bodies in the long run? How is one supposed to differentiate between good foods and bad foods? How does one find the best diet?

The answer, simply enough, lies within.

> 'When it comes to food, don't ask anyone. You must learn to ask the body and listen to it. You should eat what your body is most happy with.'
>
> – Sadhguru

Yes, but how will I know?

In the Yogic tradition, the way food is perceived goes beyond biology and chemistry. Food is alive, with a quality and *prana* (life energy) of its own. When consumed, the quality of the food influences the qualities of our body and mind. The line 'you are what you eat' takes on a whole new meaning. If we pay sufficient attention and become aware of the subtle connection shared between food and the body, we will effortlessly know from within what we need to eat and how much. We will not need to seek external sources of information. Armed with this awareness, what is merely a daily intake of food can be transformed into a beautiful process of nourishment and union. At the Isha Yoga Centre, founded by Sadhguru and located at the Velliangiri foothills in southern India, mealtime is not just about food and dining. Rather, it is approached as a possibility to touch the very source of life within.

> *The true joy of eating is that you are conscious of another life willing to become a part of you, to merge and mingle with your own life. This is the greatest pleasure that a human being knows; in some way something that is not him is willing to become a part of him. This is what you call 'love'. This is what people call 'devotion'. This is the ultimate goal of the spiritual process.'*
>
> *– Sadhguru*

It is with this very same love and devotion that we offer you this volume, in the hope that you, too, can discover the true joy of eating. *A Taste of Well-Being* is not a diet, a food doctrine, or a regimented lifestyle plan. It is a guidebook to human well-being – on all levels. In the following pages, you will find recipes that have been perfected in the kitchen of the Isha Yoga Centre and in the homes of thousands of Isha meditators across the world. Some dishes are positive-pranic adaptations of old favourites, and others might be completely new to your palate. Ranging from simple juices and salads to complete meals of grains, cereals and curries, each dish has been crafted to appeal to the taste buds and also provide wholesome nourishment.

Through pictures and testimonials, you can also get a glimpse into life at the Isha Yoga Centre, a space designed for inner transformation, whose inhabitants have embraced the mission of bringing well-being to themselves and to all. Profound insights from Sadhguru on the process of eating, digestion, classification of foods and more are peppered throughout the book.

This book is a means for you to bring a true 'taste of well-being' into your home. Whether it finds a permanent place in your bookshelf or on your kitchen counter, we hope that the following chapters will help you discover the potential – both gastronomically and spiritually – that lies within.

Pranam,
Isha Volunteers

Note: Recipes are made for a standard serving size of four.
* denotes that there's a more detailed description of that item in the index.

Aum... Aum... Aum
Sahana vavatu sahanau bhunaktu
Sahaveeryam karavavahai
Tejasvinavadhitamastu
Mavid visha vahai
Aum... Shanti Shanti Shantihi

Let us be together. Let us eat together.
Let us produce energy together.
Let there be no limit to our energies.
Let there be no ill-feeling among us.
Aum... Peace, Peace, Peace.

'This is an invocation in Sanskrit to prepare yourself in a certain way. You don't have to know its meaning. If you simply utter the sound, it creates a certain situation within you. We are not saying this to thank God, but to create an inner situation where we receive food with a certain sense of respect, understanding and reverence.

By eating, you are performing the tremendous act of transforming this food – which was mud at one time, which became a plant at another time, and which is now here on your plate – into a human being. It is not a small job. It is a big evolutionary step. You are transforming mud into human nature, and if you are willing, you can transform this mud into Divine nature within yourself.

The only god who is really sustaining you is food. We refer to food as a goddess – Annapurna. It is not that some goddess sitting somewhere is giving us food. We say 'Annam Brahmam' – the food itself is God. All other gods you have known only in your mind. In real experience, the air that you breathe, the earth that you walk upon, and the food that you eat are the gods who are sustaining you every moment.'

– *Sadhguru*

Banana Stem Juice

Hibiscus Flower Tea

Wheat
Coffee

Ginger
Coriander
Coffee

Beans and
Corn Salad

Broccoli
Cucumber
Salad

Palak and Fruit Salad

Carrot Crunch

At the Isha Yoga Centre, each meal begins with an invocation (p.xvii). This helps to create a conducive atmosphere within you so that you can receive the food and the nourishment it provides in the best possible way.

In our tradition, serving spiritual seekers and monks has always been of utmost importance. This can be a path in itself. The most beautiful expression of this is the Annadanam – the sacred offering of food.
SADHGURU

At the Isha Yoga Centre, two meals are served for ashram volunteers every day in Biksha Hall (dining hall) at 10 a.m. and 7 p.m. Thousands of people sit cross-legged on the ground and partake of this offering in complete silence.

*Kavuni
Arisi Kanji*

*Kambu and
Ragi Kali with
Moar Kuzhambu*

$\mathcal{P}ositive$
$\mathcal{P}ranic\ \mathcal{F}oods$

$\mathcal{Z}ero$
$\mathcal{P}ranic\ \mathcal{F}oods$

$\mathcal{N}egative$
$\mathcal{P}ranic\ \mathcal{F}oods$

Akshaya (the Isha Kitchen) is a perpetually busy place. On a regular day, it serves sixty separate items to around 3500 people, catering to different groups at the Isha Yoga Centre. There are distinct menus for Brahmacharis, ashram volunteers, programme participants, Isha Home School and Isha Samskriti students, guests and visitors. On Sunday visits and during residential yoga programmes which bring in an additional thousand people, about a hundred items are prepared, while special events like Mahashivaratri call for ninety different items for up to 30,000 diners.

Banana Flower
Dal Fry

Aviyal

*Groundnut
Capsicum
Subzi*

*Pakoda
Kuzhambu*

The dinner that breaks the Ekadashi fast at Isha Yoga Centre.

*Appam with
Coconut Milk*

*Green Dosa
with Chutney
and Sambar*

*Bottle
Gourd
Muthiya*

Drumstick Chutney,
Butter Fruit
Chutney and Toovar
Dal Chutney

Banana
Roti

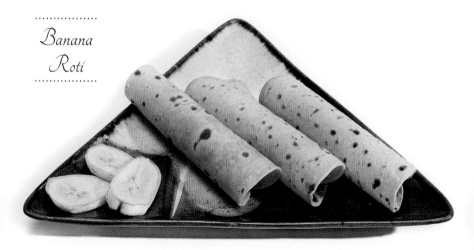

Date
Balls

Ash Gourd
Halwa

Coconut
Mango Crisp

An aerial view of the Isha Yoga Centre, set against the backdrop of the Velliangiri Mountains.

Master chef. A refined gourmet, Sadhguru pays attention to every spice and ingredient comprising a meal. If you ever get to sample something he has cooked, be prepared for an explosion of taste and a lifelong enslavement of tongue.

A selection of lentils, spices and grains

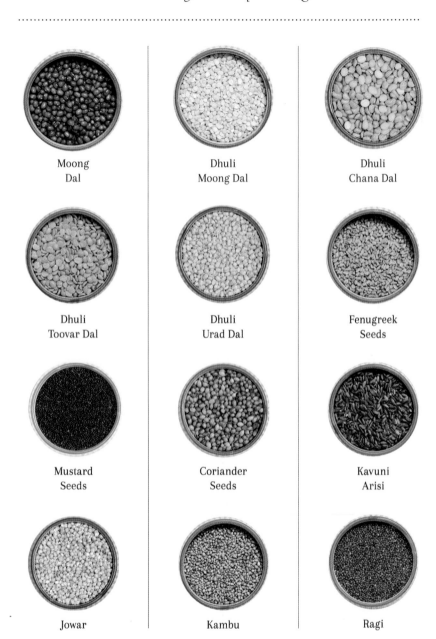

Moong
Dal

Dhuli
Moong Dal

Dhuli
Chana Dal

Dhuli
Toovar Dal

Dhuli
Urad Dal

Fenugreek
Seeds

Mustard
Seeds

Coriander
Seeds

Kavuni
Arisi

Jowar

Kambu

Ragi

Juices and Teas

In this section, you'll find some tasty and refreshing beverages. Before you dive in, please note:

- The ingredients listed for all juices are approximate and can be adjusted as per individual taste.
- For most drinks, honey – a healthier ingredient – can be used to replace sugar or palm sugar.
- While somewhat chilled juices are pleasant on hot days, Ayurveda advises against drinking ice-cold drinks as they hinder digestion.

Lemon Mint Juice

• •

INGREDIENTS
2 lemons
14–16 mint leaves, fresh
Honey / palm sugar / sugar to taste

METHOD
1. Blend the lemon juice and the mint leaves together in a blender.
2. Add the honey (or other sweetener) along with 4 cups of water.
3. Blend it well together. Strain the juice.
4. Pour the juice into glasses and serve chilled.

• *Rolling the lemons on a hard surface before cutting will ensure maximum juice yield.*
• *Blending the mint leaves whole allows for more flavour to be released into the juice.*

Carrot–Pear Juice

• •

INGREDIENTS
5 carrots, large, peeled, roughly chopped
4 pears, peeled, roughly chopped, seeds and pips removed
Honey / palm sugar / sugar to taste

METHOD
1. Blend the carrots, pears, and honey (or any other sweetener) together with 4 cups of water until smooth. (Some prefer to strain the juice for a smooth texture, but in doing so, much of the fibre and nutrients get lost. To ensure the drink is smooth, start blending with a minimal amount of water, and add more as it blends.)
2. Pour the juice into glasses and serve chilled.

Papaya Juice

• •

INGREDIENTS
½ (approx. ¼ kg) papaya*, peeled, seeds removed, chopped
½ (approx. ¼ kg) musk melon, peeled, seeds removed, chopped
Honey / palm sugar / sugar to taste

METHOD
1. Put both the papaya and musk melon in a blender or food processor.
2. Add 4 cups of water and honey (or any other sweetener). Blend well together.
3. Pour the juice into glasses and serve chilled.

3

Grape and Mixed Fruit Juice

•••

INGREDIENTS
500 g black grapes, seedless
8–10 cashews, broken
2 pieces (each 1"-thick) pineapple, fresh, finely chopped
2 apples, finely chopped
Honey / palm sugar / sugar to taste

METHOD
1. Extract the juice from the grapes by putting them in a blender or a food processer and then filtering.
2. Soak the cashews in hot water for 10 minutes. Drain and grind into a fine paste by putting them into a grinder or food processor with a little water.
3. Add the grape juice into the cashew paste. Add honey (or any other sweetener) and stir until the paste is dissolved.
4. Pour the juice into glasses and serve chilled, topped with pineapple and apple bits.

• *Use the 'start-stop' technique when grinding the cashews to avoid them becoming too greasy. Add a little water in between so the cashew paste is not too thick.*

Banana Stem Juice

• •

INGREDIENTS
2 (approx. 200 g) banana stems*
1"-piece ginger, peeled, chopped
¼ cup curd
6–8 curry leaves
2–3 coriander leaves, fresh, chopped
Salt to taste

METHOD
1. Remove the outer layer of the banana stem up to the core, where there are no more layers to remove. Finely chop the inner part, simultaneously removing the hanging fibres. As you cut the inner stem into pieces, put the cut pieces into water diluted with buttermilk – or in water mixed with lime juice – to ensure that the pieces do not change colour. (If they are cut and kept separately, they turn brown in colour.)
2. Put the banana stem pieces and ginger in a blender.
3. Add the curd, curry leaves, and salt. Blend well together. Add about 4 cups of water and blend again until smooth.
4. Pass the contents through a strainer.
5. Pour the juice into glasses and serve garnished with coriander leaves, either at room temperature or chilled.

• *Use the edge of a spoon instead of a vegetable peeler to effectively remove the ginger skin from rough corners.*

5

Cucumber Mint Juice

••

INGREDIENTS
1 cucumber, medium-sized, peeled, chopped into quarter pieces
1 cup curd
4–6 mint leaves, fresh
Salt to taste

METHOD
1. Put the cucumber in a blender and add the curd, salt, and about 1 cup water. Blend until smooth.
2. Pour the juice into glasses and serve chilled, topped with scissor-cut mint leaves.

- *Grating the cucumber will remove the natural juice from the cucumber – instead chop into quarter-sized pieces.*
- *For a dairy-free drink, eliminate the curd.*

Cantaloupe—Banana Smoothie

• •

INGREDIENTS
1 cantaloupe melon (musk melon), small, halved, seeds removed, peeled, chopped
2 ripe bananas, peeled, sliced
2 cups coconut milk*
1 cup honey / palm sugar / sugar

METHOD
1. Put both the cantaloupe and bananas into a blender. Blend until smooth.
2. Add the coconut milk and honey (or any other sweetener); blend it all together.
3. Pour the smoothie into glasses and serve chilled.

• *This smoothie can be served by frosting the glasses with palm sugar. Moisten the outside rim of the glass with a slice of banana. Fill a saucer with palm sugar and put the rim of the glass into the sugar while slowly turning it, so only the outside edge of the glass is covered. Shake off the extra sugar and pour the smoothie into the glass.*

Jackfruit Cool Shake

INGREDIENTS
6 pieces ripe jackfruit*, chopped
½ cup jaggery*
8–10 cashews, broken
2 cups coconut milk*

METHOD
1. Make a jaggery syrup and allow to cool. *(See 'Jaggery – The Medicinal Sugar' in the 'Techniques' section.)*
2. Grind the cashews to a fine paste by putting them into a grinder or food processor with a little water.
3. Blend the ripe jackfruit with the cashew paste and coconut milk until smooth. Add the jaggery syrup to taste. For better consistency, blend the jackfruit with the cashew paste first. As they blend well together, add the coconut milk and jaggery syrup.
4. Serve garnished with cashews.

• *Use the 'start-stop' technique when grinding the cashews to avoid them becoming too greasy. Add a little water in between so that the cashew paste is not too thick.*

8

Tangy Mango Lassi

INGREDIENTS
1 raw mango, peeled, grated
2 cups curd
1½ tsp cumin* seeds
1 tsp black salt
2 tsp sugar
6–8 mint leaves, fresh
Salt to taste

METHOD
1. Cook the mango in a pan with 1 cup of water until soft. Allow to cool completely.
2. Blend the cooked mango with curd. Add the cumin seeds, black salt, sugar, and salt. Blend well together. For a thick, milkshake-

* For best presentation, chill the lassi in a refrigerator again before serving. This will allow the curd to reset and stay thick.
* Full of fresh fruit and rich in calcium, lassi is the quintessential beverage to revive the spirit on hot summer days. Lassis come in many varieties, and each person can develop their own favourite recipe.
* This recipe yields a salty, tangy lassi. For a purely sweet lassi, use ripe mangoes. Add slivers of almond, cardamom, saffron strands, and/or honey to taste while blending. If desired, 1 tsp of rose water can also be stirred in before serving.

like texture, allow the drink to be whipped up well, either in the blender or by hand.

3. Pour the *lassi* into glasses and serve chilled, garnished with hand-torn mint leaves on top.

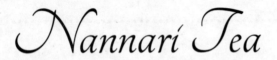

Nannari Tea

INGREDIENTS
5 (1"-piece) *nannari* roots*
1 green cardamom* pod
Honey / palm jaggery* to taste

METHOD
1. Dry the nannari roots in the shade. When fully dried, grind to powder with the cardamom pod. (This powder can be stored in a dry, airtight container for further use.)
2. Bring 4 cups of water to the boil in a pot. Add the nannari powder; lower heat and simmer for at least 2–3 minutes. Remove from heat and strain.
3. Add honey / palm jaggery to taste. Serve hot.

Lemongrass Ginger Tea

• •

INGREDIENTS
2–3 lemongrass*
½"-piece ginger, fresh, washed, chopped into roundels without peeling
Honey / jaggery* to taste

METHOD
1. Bring 4 cups of water to boil in a pot. Add the lemongrass and ginger; boil on high heat. When it comes to boil, reduce heat to low, and let it continue to simmer until the water turns light brown.
2. Remove the pot from heat and cover it. Allow it to sit for 10-15 minutes.
3. Strain the liquid, squeezing the lemongrass and ginger pieces to ensure maximum flavour is released. Allow the water to cool completely before storing in the refrigerator.
4. Add the honey / jaggery to taste. Stir and serve immediately.

- *If the ginger skin is retained, ensure that it is thoroughly washed before boiling.*
- *Honey should never be consumed cooked as it turns slightly toxic. Ensure it is added only at the end, just before drinking.*
- *This tea can be served hot or cool. If desired, a dash of lemon juice can also be added before serving.*
- *Instead of preparing the tea fresh from lemongrass stalks, a few drops of lemongrass oil can be mixed with hot water and honey/jaggery.*

Cinnamon Tea

••

INGREDIENTS
1 (2"-long) cinnamon* stick
½"-piece ginger, fresh, washed, cut into roundels without peeling
Honey / palm jaggery* to taste

METHOD
1. Bring 4 cups of water to boil in a pot. Add the cinnamon stick and ginger; boil on high heat for 5 minutes.
2. Remove the pot from the heat and cover it. Allow it to sit for about half an hour.
3. Strain the liquid, squeezing the cinnamon stick and ginger pieces to ensure that maximum flavour is released. (Allow the water to cool completely before storing in the refrigerator.)
4. Add the honey / palm jaggery to taste. Stir and serve immediately.

- *If the ginger skin is retained, ensure it is thoroughly washed before boiling.*
- *Alternately, 2 tsp of cinnamon powder can be used instead of the cinnamon stick. If so, use a cloth to strain the liquid. If desired, clove can also be added.*
- *Squeeze a couple of slices of fresh orange for a sweet twist, or a little lemon for a citrus flavour.*

Hibiscus Flower Tea

••

INGREDIENTS
1 cup dried hibiscus* flowers *(ensure the flowers are edible and not treated with chemicals or pesticides)*
1 (1"-long) cinnamon* stick
½"-piece ginger, fresh, washed, cut into roundels without removing skin
Honey / palm jaggery* to taste

METHOD
1. Bring 4 cups of water to boil in a pot. Add the hibiscus flowers, cinnamon stick, and ginger pieces; boil for 5 minutes.
2. Remove the pot from the heat and cover it. Allow it to sit for 15–20 minutes. (Keeping the flowers in water longer may result in a bitter taste. For more flavour you can add more dried flowers into the water instead.)
3. Strain the liquid, squeezing the cinnamon sticks and ginger pieces to ensure maximum flavour is released.
4. Add honey / palm jaggery to taste. Serve either hot or cold. Allow the water to cool completely before storing in the refrigerator.

- *Alternately, 1 tsp of cinnamon powder can be used instead of the cinnamon stick. If so, use a cloth to strain the liquid.*
- *This tea is often served cold by refrigerating after step 4, garnished with a few mint leaves or a slice of lemon.*

Rose Petal Flower Tea

INGREDIENTS
1½ cups rose petals* *(ensure the flowers are edible and not treated with chemicals or pesticides)*
2 green cardamom* pods
Honey / palm jaggery* to taste

METHOD
1. Bring 4 cups of water to boil in a pot. Add the rose petals and green cardamom pods; boil for 5 minutes.
2. Remove the pot from the heat and cover it. Allow it to sit for 15-20 minutes.
3. Strain the liquid, squeezing the flowers and cardamom pods to ensure maximum flavour is released. Add the honey / palm jaggery. Serve hot.

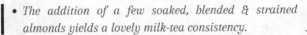
• *The addition of a few soaked, blended & strained almonds yields a lovely milk-tea consistency.*

Ginger Tea

∙∙

INGREDIENTS
2"-piece ginger, fresh, peeled, sliced into thin slices
25–30 *tulsi* leaves*, torn in half
2 tsp dried coriander seeds* (optional)
1 tsp lemon juice
Honey / palm jaggery* to taste

METHOD
1. Bring 4 cups of water to boil in a pot. Add ginger, tulsi leaves, and the coriander seeds, if using; lower heat and simmer for at least 2–3 minutes. Remove from heat and strain.
2. Add the lemon juice and honey / palm jaggery to taste. Serve hot.

• *Use the edge of a spoon instead of a vegetable peeler to effectively remove the ginger skin from rough corners.*
• *This tea can also be served chilled.*

Wheat Coffee

● ●

INGREDIENTS
500 g wheat kernels
50 g coriander seeds*
Milk as desired
Sugar / jaggery* to taste

METHOD
1. Dry roast the wheat kernels in a wok on medium heat. Roast them like coffee beans until they turn brown and smell good. While roasting, do not allow them to char.
2. Dry roast the coriander seeds the same way, until they smell good and become brown in colour.
3. Cool and powder both the wheat and coriander seeds together. (This powder can be stored in a dry, airtight container for further use.)
4. Bring 4 cups of water to boil. Add this 'wheat coffee' powder; lower heat, and simmer for 2-3 minutes. Remove from heat and strain.
5. Add the milk and sugar / jaggery; stir well. Serve hot.

- *Instead of wheat, you can use ragi* and / or corn. Roast them separately and powder them together.*
- *Instead of milk, you can add non-dairy milk, soy milk or coconut milk*.*

Ginger Coriander Coffee (Sukku Coffee)

••

INGREDIENTS
2"-piece ginger, crushed slightly
4 tsp coriander* seeds
Palm jaggery* to taste

METHOD
1. Bring 4 cups of water to boil. Add the ginger and coriander seeds; lower heat and simmer for 3–4 minutes. Remove from heat and strain.
2. Add the palm jaggery and stir until it dissolves. Serve hot.

• *Milk can be added, if desired.*

"

'My daughter Raika and I
returned from our stay at the Isha
Yoga Centre, refreshed and radiant. We owe our
fine fettle to the location, amidst the scenic Velliangiri
foothills, the well-constructed programme for head and soul
and, of course, the wholesome and carefully balanced diet that
sustained us throughout.

Each meal was a pleasant surprise. Without spice, the delicate
natural flavouring greatly suited our palates. The fresh vegetable
and fruit juices enlivened our spirits and did what they are meant
to do – make up for any vitamin and mineral deficiencies. Above
all else, we had the satisfaction of knowing that we were being
served healthy, non-toxic, organically grown vegetables and
fruit, caringly nurtured in the lush green fields within the
campus. The variety of vegetables, including the leafy ones,
were astonishing. In short, we re-learned our way to
healthy living and are striving to emulate the
nutritious Isha gastronomy in our home.'

– PHEROZA J. GODREJ

"

Natural Food

Sadhguru

When you eat food uncooked, in its 'live form', the life energies can be easily imbibed into your own system. It is best to eat as much 'live food' as possible because a live cell has everything within itself to sustain life. If you consume a live cell, which has the life potential in the form of a seed, you will see that it sustains the life within you very well and brings a different sense of aliveness in your body – an alertness which cooked food cannot bring.

The nature of cooked food is lethargy. Traditionally in India, any cooked food prepared at home went straight from the stove to the plate. It had to be eaten within one and half hours. If the food has been cooked earlier than that, if I had a choice, I will not eat it. If you eat this kind of food, you may sleep up to 10-12 hours per day because it contains so much inertia. Today, food is kept in a refrigerator for a month or more and then consumed. This is a wrong way to eat. It is not just about increasing your sleep quota; high-inertia food will dull your mental agility and alertness and bring many other problems to your body. If you bring a little awareness into yourself, when you feel the food that comes on to your plate, you will know how much inertia it has and whether to eat it or not.

When eating raw food, you will see the sense of health in your system will be very different from anything that you have known. If you make your diet at least 50 per cent 'live' by including vegetables (those which can be eaten raw), fruits, nuts and sprouted gram, you will see that it will make a huge difference in your energy levels in so many ways. One thing that will immediately happen is that your sleep quota will go down dramatically. If you are sleeping eight hours a day, you will find that sleeping two or three hours a day will be more than enough.

Salads

The array of fruit and vegetable salads in this section will definitely keep you alert, energized and on your toes! Also, check out 'The Simplicity of Salad' in the 'Techniques' section which has easy tips for making great salads and a variety of dressings.

Green Gram Sprout Salad

INGREDIENTS

½ cup sprouted green gram *(moong dal)*,* washed, drained
(See 'Sprouts – the Power Food' in the 'Techniques' section)
4 dates, seedless, chopped
2 tbsp raisins, chopped
1–2 carrots, peeled, grated
1 tbsp coconut, grated
A dash of olive oil
Honey to taste
Lemon juice to taste

METHOD

1. Mix the sprouts, dates, raisins, carrots and coconut together in a deep bowl.
2. In a separate bowl, mix lemon juice, olive oil and honey together to make the dressing.
3. Pour the dressing over the sprouts mixture and mix thoroughly. Serve.

- *Instead of lemon juice, you can use orange or pomegranate juice.*
- *This green gram salad can be made in numerous ways. Pineapple pieces, pomegranate and dried fruit can be added for a sweet salad.*
- *For a salty salad: cucumber, tomato, raw mango or mint leaves can be added.*

Beans and Corn Salad

• •

INGREDIENTS

1½ cups red kidney beans *(rajma)*,* uncooked
8–10 baby corn, washed, chopped into ½" rounds
¼ cabbage, small, shredded
½ green capsicum, medium-sized, deseeded, diced into small pieces
2 tomatoes, small, finely chopped
1 cucumber, small, peeled, chopped into small pieces
1 carrot, small, peeled, chopped into small pieces
5 olives, halved
½ lemon
1½ tsp olive oil
1 tsp roasted cumin*, powdered
2 sprigs coriander leaves, fresh, finely chopped
Salt to taste
Black pepper powder to taste

• *The kidney beans can be cooked by washing well in a colander, then soaking overnight. In the morning, drain the water and add the kidney beans along with fresh water into a pot and boil for 10-15 minutes. Then bring to a simmer and let it cook for another 90-120 minutes. An easy way to check if they are ready is if you press the beans, they should be tender, but not mushy. If the beans are still crunchy, then allow them to cook at a simmer for some more time, checking if they are ready every 10 minutes.*

METHOD

1. Cook the kidney beans *(See tip)*.
2. Put the kidney beans, baby corn, cabbage, capsicum, tomato, cucumber, carrot, and olives in a deep bowl. Toss once or twice.
3. In a separate bowl, mix the juice of the lemon with olive oil, salt, black pepper powder, and roasted cumin powder.
4. Pour the dressing over the salad and toss well. Serve garnished with coriander leaves.

Sweet Corn Salad

• •

INGREDIENTS

1 cup sweet corn kernels (or 2 ears of sweet corn)
2 tomatoes, medium-sized, halved, deseeded, finely chopped
1 green capsicum, medium-sized, halved, deseeded, finely chopped
1 cucumber, medium-sized, peeled, finely chopped
7–8 black olives, finely chopped
50 g iceberg lettuce, shredded into small pieces
¼ cup mint leaves, fresh, shredded into small pieces
½ lemon
1 tbsp olive oil
2–3 sprigs coriander leaves, fresh, finely chopped
Salt to taste
Black pepper powder to taste

METHOD

1. Cook the corn *(See tip)*.
2. Put the corn, tomatoes, capsicum, cucumber, olives, lettuce and mint leaves in a bowl.
3. In a separate bowl, mix the juice of the lemon with olive oil, salt and pepper powder.
4. Pour the dressing over the salad and toss well. Serve garnished with coriander leaves.

• *Boil or grill (grilled corn yields maximum flavour) the ears of corn for 6-9 minutes. For added flavour, butter or oil the ears of corn. Use a knife to remove the corn kernels by holding the stem of the corn cob to the bottom of a large bowl. This way, the natural liquid from the cob will also be used.*
• *If using fresh sweet corn kernels, boil with 2 cups of water. Cook for 3-4 minutes and drain. Allow it to cool.*

Chickpea (Chana) Chaat Delight

∙∙∙

INGREDIENTS
1 cup chickpeas *(kabuli chana)**
1 tomato, medium-sized, chopped
1 green capsicum, medium-sized, halved, deseeded, finely chopped
1 cucumber, small, peeled, finely chopped
¼ cabbage, small, shredded with knife
½ lemon
2 tsp *chaat masala**
Salt to taste

- *The chickpeas can be cooked by washing well in a colander, then soaking overnight. In the morning, drain the water and add the chickpeas along with fresh water into a pot and boil for 10-15 minutes. Then bring to a simmer and let it cook for another 90-120 minutes. An easy way to check if they are ready is if you press the chickpeas, they should be tender, but not mushy. If the chickpeas are still crunchy, then allow them to simmer for some more time, checking if they are ready every 10 minutes.*
- *Keep the dressing aside until just before serving to ensure that the vegetables remain crisp and fresh.*
- *Dressing can be enhanced and altered by adding various ingredients like some zest of orange or lemon, different herbs, vinegar or masalas.*

METHOD
1. Cook the chickpeas *(See tip)*.
2. Put the cooked chickpeas, tomato, capsicum, cucumber, and cabbage in a deep bowl.
3. In a separate bowl, mix the juice of the lemon with the chaat masala and salt.
4. Drizzle the dressing onto the salad and toss all the ingredients well together. Serve immediately.

Broccoli– Cucumber Salad

••

INGREDIENTS
1 head broccoli florets
2 cucumbers, peeled, chopped into ½"-square pieces
2 tomatoes, chopped
1 green capsicum, chopped
1 head iceberg lettuce, torn into bite-sized pieces
½ lemon
4–5 mint leaves, fresh
2 tbsp olive oil
6–8 sprigs coriander leaves, fresh, chopped
Salt to taste
Black pepper powder to taste

METHOD
1. Boil the broccoli florets in water for 3-4 minutes (or until the broccoli just turns bright green); drain. Rinse the broccoli in cold water to prevent it from cooking further (also known as blanching). Chop into smaller pieces.

- *For flavour, add a dash of salt into the water when boiling the broccoli florets.*
- *Sprinkle roasted walnuts, sesame seeds, pine nuts, sunflower seeds, sliced almonds, cashews or raisins to the salad before serving, if desired.*

2. Put the cucumbers, tomatoes, capsicum, broccoli and lettuce in a deep bowl.
3. Blend the lemon juice, mint leaves, olive oil, salt and pepper powder in the blender to a smooth consistency. Water may be added to create a salad dressing-like consistency.
4. Add the dressing to the bowl of vegetables and toss well. Serve garnished with fresh coriander.

Pasta Salad

• •

INGREDIENTS
½ cup fusilli (spiral pasta)
4–5 broccoli florets
1 tomato, large, halved, deseeded, finely chopped
1 yellow capsicum, medium-sized, halved, deseeded, finely chopped
1 cucumber, medium-sized, peeled, finely chopped
7–8 black olives, quartered
60 g cottage cheese *(paneer)**, chopped into small cubes
½ lemon
2 tbsp olive oil
8–10 mint leaves, fresh, torn
3 sprigs coriander leaves,* fresh, chopped
Salt to taste
Black pepper powder to taste

METHOD
1. Bring 3 cups of water to boil in a pan; add the pasta and cook on medium heat until nearly done *(al dente)*. Drain and wash under cool water. Drain again. Toss the warm pasta with a little olive oil to prevent sticking.
2. Meanwhile, bring 1½ cups of water to the boil in another small pan and add the broccoli florets. Cook for 4–5 minutes (or until the broccoli just turns bright green); drain. Rinse in cold water to prevent it from cooking further (also known as blanching). Chop into smaller pieces.
3. Put the pasta, broccoli, tomato, capsicum, cucumber, olives and cottage cheese in a bowl. Toss once lightly.
4. In a separate bowl, mix the juice of the lemon with olive oil, salt, and pepper powder.
5. Pour the dressing over the salad and toss well. Add the mint leaves and coriander leaves; toss once more. Serve.

Beetroot Lemon Relish

•••

INGREDIENTS

2 beetroots, washed, peeled, finely grated
½ cup raw groundnuts, soaked *(See the 'Techniques' section)*
3" piece raw mango, grated
2" piece coconut, fresh, grated
½ lemon
½ tsp black pepper powder
2 sprigs coriander leaves*, fresh
Salt to taste

For the Seasoning

1 tsp oil
¼ tsp mustard seeds
¼ tsp split Bengal gram *(dhuli chana dal)**
¼ tsp split black gram, skinless *(dhuli urad dal)**
7-8 curry leaves

METHOD

1. Keep the grated beetroot aside in a deep bowl. If you want the salad with less liquid, put the grated beetroot in a clean muslin cloth and lightly squeeze to remove the juice. This juice can be reserved for later use in juices or salad dressings.

• *Add the salty lemon dressing just before serving to keep the beetroot crisp.*

2. For the seasoning, heat the oil in a small pan; add the mustard seeds, Bengal gram, black gram and curry leaves. Sauté on medium heat for half a minute, and as the grams begin to change colour, remove from heat and add this seasoning to the grated beetroot. Toss well together.
3. Add the soaked groundnuts, mango and coconut to the beetroot.
4. In a separate bowl, mix the juice of the lemon with salt and pepper powder. Toss this dressing with the salad.
5. Serve immediately garnished with chopped coriander leaves.

Sweet
Apple Salad

••

INGREDIENTS
2 apples, medium-sized, washed, chopped into small squares
½ cup coconut, grated
¼ cup *chikki* (groundnut candy)
¼ cup raisins
Honey to taste

METHOD
1. Mix the apples with the coconut, and chikki in a bowl.
2. Add the honey, toss well and serve.

Pumpkin Salad

....

INGREDIENTS
180 g yellow pumpkin, grated
¼ cup jaggery*
½ coconut, fresh, grated
1 tsp green cardamom* powder

METHOD
1. Put the grated pumpkin in a clean muslin cloth and lightly squeeze to remove some of the juice. Transfer to a deep bowl.
2. Use the jaggery to make a syrup and allow it to cool. *(See 'Jaggery – The Medicinal Sugar' in the 'Techniques' section.)*
3. Sprinkle the coconut and cardamom powder over the grated pumpkin.
4. Pour the jaggery syrup as desired.
5. Mix all the ingredients well together and serve immediately.

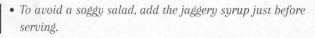

- *To avoid a soggy salad, add the jaggery syrup just before serving.*

Veggie Boost

• •

INGREDIENTS

3 tomatoes, halved, seeds discarded, chopped into ½"-square pieces
2 yellow zucchinis, cut into ½"-square pieces
½ head iceberg lettuce, torn into bite-sized pieces
2 cups Chinese cabbage, chopped, cut into ½"-square pieces
Lemon juice to taste
Olive oil to taste
Salt to taste
Black pepper powder to taste

METHOD

1. Put the tomatoes, zucchini, lettuce and Chinese cabbage in a deep bowl.
2. In a separate bowl, mix the lemon juice, olive oil, salt and pepper powder.
3. Pour the dressing over the salad and toss well. Serve.

• *Iceberg lettuce can be replaced with any other greens, such as spinach. Quantities can vary as per an individual's preference.*

Palak and Mushroom Salad

• •

INGREDIENTS
3 cups baby spinach leaves *(palak)*, washed, dried, stems removed
16–18 button mushrooms, medium-sized, washed, halved
2 cucumbers, peeled, chopped into small pieces
3 tomatoes, finely chopped
½ lemon
2 tbsp olive oil
Salt to taste
Black pepper powder to taste

METHOD
1. If desired, cook the mushrooms lightly until brown with oil, pepper, and any herb.
2. Tear the spinach leaves into bite-sized pieces and place in a deep bowl with the mushrooms.
3. Add the cucumbers and tomatoes to the bowl.
4. In a separate bowl, mix the juice of the lemon, olive oil, salt and pepper powder.
5. Pour the dressing over the salad and toss well. Serve.

• *As mushrooms often carry particles of mud, you can use a wet cloth to gently wipe the mushrooms clean.*

Palak and Fruit Salad

• •

INGREDIENTS
3 cups baby spinach leaves (palak), washed, chopped into medium-sized pieces
1 cucumber, small, washed, peeled (optional), chopped into small squares
1 apple, small, washed, peeled (optional), chopped into small squares
¼ cup cashews, chopped
¼ cup roasted groundnuts, chopped
2–3 sprigs coriander leaves*, fresh, chopped
1 orange, small, peeled, segments separated and seeds removed
¼ cup raisins

'Sweet Salad' Dressing
See 'The Simplicity of Salad' under the 'Techniques' section for the ingredients and method for making this dressing.

METHOD
1. Put all the ingredients mentioned except the last two in a deep bowl.
2. Prepare the 'Sweet Salad' dressing.
3. Mix the dressing with the mixture in the bowl.
4. Lastly, add the raisins and orange segments. Toss well and serve.

Caribbean Salad

● ●

INGREDIENTS

1 cucumber, large, washed, peeled, chopped into 1"-long pieces
2 ripe bananas, thinly sliced into 1"-long pieces
½ cup capsicum, chopped into 1"-long pieces
2 oranges, peeled, each segment halved
½ cup roasted almonds, chopped
½ cup curd

METHOD

1. Put all the ingredients except the banana pieces in a deep bowl.
   Mix well.
2. Add the bananas and toss.

• *Sesame seeds, groundnuts or any other nut can be added*
  to this salad.

Rose Salad

....

INGREDIENTS
2 cucumbers, peeled, cut into small cubes
½ pineapple, chopped into small pieces
3 edible roses *(ensure the flowers are not treated with chemicals or pesticides)*
½ lemon
10–12 mint leaves, fresh, torn
Salt to taste
Black pepper powder to taste

METHOD
1. Put the cucumber and pineapple in a deep bowl.
2. In a separate bowl, mix the juice of the lemon with salt and pepper powder.
3. Pour the dressing over the cucumber and pineapple and toss well.
4. Pluck the petals off the roses and add to the salad bowl.
5. Add mint leaves to the bowl.
6. Toss the salad well and serve.

Carrot Crunch

• •

INGREDIENTS
1 carrot, large, washed, peeled, finely chopped
1 apple, medium-sized, washed, chopped into small squares
½ cup pineapple, chopped
¼ cup raisins / dates, chopped into small pieces
¼ cup roasted groundnuts, chopped into small pieces
½ cup coconut, grated
¼ cup roasted sesame seeds

'Sweet Salad' Dressing

See 'The Simplicity of Salad' under the 'Techniques' section for
the ingredients and method for making this dressing.

METHOD
1. Mix the carrot, apple, pineapple, raisins / dates, and groundnuts
    in a deep bowl.
2. Prepare the 'Sweet Salad' dressing.
3. Add the dressing, the grated coconut, and sesame seeds to the
    mixture in the bowl. Toss well and serve.

Sweet Milky Salad

• •

INGREDIENTS

6 tsp condensed milk
2 apples, chopped with peel into ½"-square pieces
½ pineapple, fresh, chopped into ½"-square pieces
4 bananas, peeled, halved, chopped into bite-sized rounds
1 cup grapes, seedless, halved
15–20 cashews, broken

METHOD

1. Pour the condensed milk in a deep bowl.
2. Add the apple and pineapple to the condensed milk; stir once or twice. (Adding the apple to the condensed milk first will ensure the apple does not discolour.)
3. Add the bananas to the bowl and mix once.
4. Add the grapes and cashews to the bowl.
5. Mix everything well together and serve.

• *Mangoes, chikoos, berries and dry fruits also go well in this salad.*
• *You can add almonds, pistachios or saffron to the salad before serving, and it can even be served with a couple of scoops of vanilla or saffron ice cream.*

Banana Fruit Salad

••

INGREDIENTS
3 ripe bananas, peeled, chopped into 1" rounds
1 papaya*, peeled, chopped into bite-sized pieces
4 *chikoos** (sapota), halved, deseeded, quartered
1 tsp honey (optional)
15–20 mint leaves, fresh

METHOD
1. Put the bananas, papaya, and chikoos in a deep bowl.
2. Pour the honey and add the mint leaves.
3. Mix and serve.

- *Wash the papaya gently but thoroughly before cutting.*
- *If the mint leaves are large, you can 'chiffonade' them; that is, roll the leaves tightly together and cut them into strip-like pieces.*
- *If the fruits are ripe enough, honey can be omitted. If desired, grated coconut, groundnuts, and grapes can also be added.*

Apple and Pineapple Salad

• •

INGREDIENTS
2 apples, medium-sized, washed, chopped into squares
1 cup pineapple, chopped
10–12 mint leaves, fresh, torn
Lemon juice to taste
Honey to taste

METHOD
1. Mix all the ingredients well together and serve.

• *If desired, the 'Sweet Salad' dressing in the 'The Simplicity of Salad' under the 'Techniques' section can be prepared and added instead of lemon juice and honey.*

Peanut Butter-Banana Salad

••

INGREDIENTS
2 bananas, cut lengthwise
½ cup peanut butter
2 tbsp lemon juice
1 cup lettuce, shredded
½ cup groundnuts, roasted, chopped
Honey to taste

METHOD
1. Mix the peanut butter and honey well in a bowl.
2. Dip the bananas into the lemon juice.
3. Place the banana halves on the shredded lettuce.
4. Spread the peanut butter mixture over the bananas.
5. Sprinkle with groundnuts. Serve.

Inside 'Akshaya' – The Isha Kitchen

Inside Akshaya, the Isha Kitchen, there is a mad passion to prepare and serve the most nutritious and tasty foods to all who come for a meal. Swami Vibodha, former head of the ashram kitchen, shares the backstage activities with a smile.

Our activity always starts with a Guru Pooja.[1] During ashram programmes, the activity starts at 4 a.m. and ends at 1 p.m. On other days, we start at 5 a.m.

We are never sure how many people need to be served until the dining time. As people eat, we prepare to make food for another 500 people. There is always a back-up team in the kitchen for any emergency.

Many ashram visitors share that they have never tasted this kind of food anywhere else. They may use the same ingredients, they may even be able to cook better technically, but when the preparation is done as an offering, the quality of the food is totally different. Sadhguru has often told us that the kind of attitude we take to prepare the food determines how the food will be.

Sometimes we get tired physically, but because it is happening out of joy, we can do it. Everything is done with such a sense of offering, and when we see the result – people having their food happily – we feel so fulfilled. Seeing this, we are so overwhelmed; we can never see this work as a burden.

Various people from different parts of the world share their

---

[1] A traditional offering and invocation performed to the Guru.

recipes with us, and we modify them a little according to the needs of the ashram. They bring new grocery items and explain their nutritional value, and we include them in the menu. Due to this we have an international variety of foods, including salads and bakery items. We are constantly learning new recipes. It is so wonderful that people from all over the world are helping in Akshaya.

"

'Biksha is an ancient Indian tradition
as per which ascetics and sadhus go door to
door, asking for food and alms from people. It is, in
fact, a path for the spiritual seeker to absolve his/her ego,
since asking for biksha means one has to approach strangers
and ask them for alms. Giving and receiving biksha has always
played a significant role for the spiritual seeker.

Like every aspect of Isha is designed and named for the purposes it serves,
the dining hall is named The Biksha Hall, giving us meditators and others an
opportunity to experience the process of giving and receiving biksha.

From entering into the Biksha Hall with folded palms and treading on one of
the most pious places on earth, to being received by equally humble volunteers
of all ages, greeting you with folded palms and a gentle smile, one can only be
humbled. The clean and quiet environs are disturbed only by the shuffle of feet
as we sit down, cross-legged, to be served one of the most delicious spreads.

Starting with an invocation, a tradition in Isha, I normally commence
eating with tears of joy. The volunteers do not give us any opportunity
to ask for a second helping; they just appear with their little buckets
full of hot, nutritious helpings. It has always felt like a king's
meal served with utmost respect. I could only receive it in
all humility!'

– NIVEDITA RAM

"

Gruels and Grains

The carbohydrate part of our diet is very important, as it is the source of energy and metabolism. While we usually think 'carbs' mean white rice and wheat, nature offers us a plethora of highly nutritious grains that many people are missing out on. In this section, we feature some of these neglected cereals as well as some of the most delicious and nourishing carbohydrate preparations in southern India, with particular attention to *kanjis* and *kalis*.

Of Kanjis and Kalis

KANJI

Kanji is similar to a porridge or gruel, and can be made from a variety of grains and lentils. Highly nutritious and easy to digest, kanjis are a regular item at the Isha Yoga Centre, made from either *ragi*, wheat, rice, oats or *Sanjeevini*.*

Any of the following recipes can be prepared with pearl millet flour, corn flour, foxtail millet, kodo millet, little millet, wheat flour, wheat *rava*, oats or rice flour. Buttermilk is a particularly common addition to some salted kanjis, while coconut milk adds a rich taste to other sweet kanjis. Having kanji every morning for breakfast along with soaked groundnuts *(See 'Protein – Power Groundnuts' in the 'Techniques' section)* can help to keep the body active, light and energetic throughout the day.

Millets such as *jowar* (*cholam* in Tamil), pearl millet (*kambu*), finger millet (*kezhvaragu*), kodo millet (*varagu*), foxtail millet (*tinai*), proso millet (*panivaragu*), barnyard millet (*kudraivali*) and little millet (*samai*), pulses such as black, green and red grams, coconut, groundnut and sunflower constitute the main crops grown in southern India.

KALI

Kali is any grain or cereal made into paste form. Generally it is consumed with cooked vegetables, curd or any dal / *sambar*.* When the grains are consumed in liquid form, it is called kanji or gruel. Making kali or kanji a part of the diet is a simple way for vegetarians to fulfill their protein and calcium requirements.

Ragi Kanji
(Finger Millet Gruel)

• •

INGREDIENTS
2 tsp ragi* (finger millet) flour
2½ tsp powdered jaggery* / palm sugar
2 cups water

METHOD
1. In a medium saucepan, bring 1½ cups of water to a rapid boil.
2. In a separate bowl, whisk the remaining ½ cup of water into the ragi flour, making a paste. Ensure no lumps are formed.
3. Add the paste to the boiling water and stir continuously to prevent lumps from forming and to make sure the kanji does not stick to the bottom of the pan. Cook on low heat for 4-5 minutes.
4. When the raw smell disappears, add the jaggery / palm sugar and cook for 2 more minutes. Remove from heat, allow to cool and serve.

• *You can add cardamom*, almond powder, dates, cashews, raw groundnuts, dried coconut powder (copra), and/or pistachio powder to this kanji.*
• *For a salty kanji, omit the jaggery/palm sugar and use salt instead. Sour buttermilk can also be added.*

Kavuni Arisi (Black Rice) Sweet Gruel

••

INGREDIENTS

½ cup black rice *(kavuni arisi)*,* washed, soaked in 2 cups water for 2–3 hours
1 cup milk
½ cup coconut milk*
¼ cup coconut, grated
2 tsp *ghee**
5 raisins
10 cashews
2 pinches green cardamom* powder
Sugar to taste

• *This kanji can be made thick and even served as a sweet, topped with grated coconut or sliced fruits.*
• *It can also be served alongside ice cream. In this case, you can add vanilla extract, coconut cream or palm sugar.*

METHOD
1. Cook the rice along with 3 cups of water in a pressure cooker.
2. After the first whistle, lower heat and cook for about 10–15 minutes more. Remove from heat and allow it to cool. (After this step, you can change the consistency as per preference. For a drinkable porridge, make it thin by adding milk, coconut milk or water. For a thick, *halwa*-like consistency, drain the water first before adding the other ingredients.)
3. Stir the rice and gently mash.
4. Add the sugar and grated coconut. Mix well.
5. Heat the ghee in a small pan, lightly sauté the raisins and cashews until golden. Remove.
6. Add to the rice along with green cardamom powder; mix well. Serve.

Gasagasaa (Poppy Seed) Sweet Gruel

INGREDIENTS
¼ cup poppy seeds *(khus khus)*, soaked in 2 cups water for 2-3 hours, drained
½ cup sugar
2 cups milk
2 pinches green cardamom* powder
10 cashews
1 tsp ghee*

METHOD
1. Grind the poppy seeds in a mixer to a smooth paste.
2. Pour ½ cup water in a pan. Add the sugar and allow it to boil until a syrup of one-string consistency is formed (one-string consistency can be checked by lifting a ladle from the syrup. If the syrup drops in a single string – not two or three – it has reached the proper consistency).
3. Add the poppy seed paste and allow it to boil for 2-3 minutes.
4. Finally, add the milk and green cardamom powder. Boil for 4-5 minutes; remove from heat.
5. Heat the ghee in a small pan; fry the cashews till golden brown. Remove and add to the gruel.
6. Mix well and serve.

• *This porridge can even be served as payasam. In this case, thin the porridge with milk or coconut milk. Fried coconut shreds, raisins and cardamom pods can be added, along with a little ghee.*

Ragi (Finger Millet) Puttu

● ●

INGREDIENTS
1 cup ragi* (finger millet) flour
1 cup rice flour
Salt to taste

For the Seasoning

3 tsp oil
1 tsp mustard seeds
3 red chillies
12–14 curry leaves
½ coconut, fresh, grated

METHOD
1. Mix and sift the ragi flour and rice flour together into a deep bowl.
2. Add 2–3 tbsp of salted water. Mix until it reaches a crumb-like texture. Bring it to *puttu** consistency – when the dough is held, it should form a lump. When it is crushed, it should become powdery.

- *If desired, red chilli powder can be added to taste after step 5.*
- *To make wheat puttu, use wheat flour instead of rice flour.*
- *To make a sweet puttu, use normal water instead of salted water in step 2. Add grated coconut, jaggery*, ghee*, and cardamom* powder after step 4. Serve plain or with mashed bananas.*

3. Sift using a sieve with large holes. Spread the sieved dough over a wet cloth and place the cloth in an *idli** steamer. Steam for 10-15 minutes.
4. Heat half of the oil in a pan; add the cooked puttu. Sauté on medium heat for 2-3 minutes.
5. Add the coconut and mix.
6. In a separate pan, heat the remaining oil and add the mustard seeds. As they begin to splutter, add the red chillies and curry leaves.
7. Add the seasoning to the fried puttu. Stir lightly and remove from heat.
8. Serve hot with any gravy.

Ragi (Finger Millet) Kali

. . . .

INGREDIENTS
3 cups ragi* (finger millet) flour
6 cups water
Salt to taste

METHOD
1. Pour 3 cups of water in a pan and bring it to boil.
2. Meanwhile, whisk the ragi flour in 3 cups of water to a smooth paste. Add this paste to the pan and stir continuously to prevent lumps from forming, and to ensure that the paste does not stick to the bottom of the pan.
3. Cook, stirring continuously, on low heat until well-cooked, approximately 15 minutes. (The kali is cooked when it reaches a thick pudding or mashed potato-like consistency, but it should not be sticky to touch.)
4. Remove from heat, cool and make balls of it, or spread it like mashed potatoes. Serve.

Kambu (Pearl Millet) Kali

INGREDIENTS
1 cup kambu* (pearl millet) flour
5 cups water
Salt to taste

METHOD
1. Pour 2 cups of water in a bowl and soak the kambu flour for 10 minutes.
2. Add the remaining water to a pan and allow it to boil.
3. Meanwhile, whisk the kambu flour to a smooth paste. Add this paste to the pan and stir continuously to prevent lumps from forming, and to ensure that the paste does not stick to the bottom of the pan.
4. Cook, stirring continuously, on low heat until well-cooked, approximately 15 minutes. (The kali is cooked when it reaches a thick pudding or mashed potato-like consistency, but it should not be sticky to touch.)
5. Remove from heat, cool and roll it into balls, or spread it like mashed potatoes. Serve.

Urad Dal Palm Sugar Kali

INGREDIENTS
1 cup split black gram *(urad dal)* flour *(See tip)*
1 cup palm sugar / jaggery*
½ cup gingelly oil*
1 tsp cardamom* powder
2 tbsp ghee*
10 cashews

METHOD
1. Make jaggery syrup. *(See 'Jaggery – The Medicinal Sugar' in the 'Techniques' section.)*
2. Add 4 tsp gingelly oil to the syrup and whisk the black gram flour into the liquid, avoiding the formation of lumps. Sprinkle in the cardamom powder and mix well, until the flour / syrup mixture becomes a thick dough. (It is better to add the flour in small quantities in the boiling syrup. Putting the flour in the syrup all at once will result in lumps.)

* *To prepare black gram (urad dal) flour, first dry roast 500 g black gram with 50 g fenugreek seeds* and 50 g dried ginger. When it gives off a nice aroma, remove from heat and cool. Mix in 500 g raw rice. Grind these to a coarse powder. Store in an airtight bottle and use as required.*

3. Add the remaining gingelly oil into the dough in a slow trickle, stirring continuously.
4. In a separate pan, heat the ghee and roast the cashews until light brown. Add them to the dough.
5. Remove from heat when the flour is no longer sticky and leaves the sides of the pan. Allow the dough to cool. This can be served like a halwa or made into balls and served.

Moar Kali

• •

INGREDIENTS
1 cup rice flour
3 cups buttermilk
½ tsp turmeric powder*
4 tsp gingelly oil*
2 curd chillies *(moar molagai)**
½ tsp split black gram, skinless (dhuli urad dal)*
½ tsp mustard seeds
7–8 curry leaves
Salt to taste

METHOD
1. Place the rice flour into a mixing bowl. Gradually whisk in the buttermilk so that lumps are not formed. Continue stirring as you add in the salt and turmeric powder. Set aside.
2. Heat the gingelly oil in a thick-bottomed pan on low heat. Add the curd chillies and roast until they change colour. Remove immediately and set aside.
3. In the same oil, add the mustard seeds and allow them to splutter. Then add the split black gram. When it starts to change colour, add the curry leaves.
4. Pour the rice flour and buttermilk mixture into the seasoning and stir vigorously, avoiding the formation of lumps. Cook on low heat.

• *For a tangy twist to the dish, you can add a little tamarind* water to the buttermilk.*
• *If desired, drizzle a little coconut oil on the kali before serving. While the kali is delicious by itself, it can also be had with your choice of sambar*, pickle or chutney.*

5. When the consistency reaches a semi-solid paste, remove from heat. (If the batter is still sticky, it should be cooked for longer.)
6. Grease a large plate with a little oil. Pour the mixture and flatten it. Allow it to cool.
7. Cut it into small pieces. Serve cool, garnished with fried curd chillies.

Wheat Rice

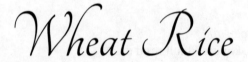

INGREDIENTS
½ cup broken wheat, washed
2 tsp oil
Salt to taste

METHOD
1. Put the broken wheat in a cooker with 1 cup water, 2 tsp oil, and a pinch of salt.
2. Close the lid and cook until 2 whistles.
3. Remove from heat and allow the pressure to be fully released.
4. Open lid and serve. Use as cooked rice.

Wheat Bisibelebhath

∙∙∙

INGREDIENTS

1 cup broken wheat, washed, soaked in 3 cups water for 10 minutes
¾ cup split pigeon peas *(dhuli toovar dal)*,* washed, soaked in 3 cups water for 10 minutes
2 carrots, medium-sized, peeled, chopped into small pieces
10–12 French beans, stringed, chopped
1 drumsticks*, trimmed, cut into 3"-pieces
½ cup green peas
½ tsp turmeric powder*
2 tsp oil
1 tsp mustard seeds
3 red chillies
8–10 curry leaves
2 tomatoes, medium-sized, chopped into small pieces
3 tbsp *bisibelebhath* powder*
1 small marble-sized ball tamarind*, soaked in ¼ cup water, juice extracted
3 tsp ghee*
10 cashews
½ cup coriander leaves*, fresh, finely chopped
Salt to taste

METHOD

1. Heat the oil in a pressure cooker; add the mustard seeds and allow them to splutter. Then add the red chillies and curry leaves; sauté for 10 seconds.

> • *This dish goes well with potato chips, papad or other crisps on the side.*
> • *Though bisibelebhath powder is readily available in shops, you can make it at home too (see recipe on next page).*

2. Add the tomatoes and bisibelebhath powder; sauté until a pleasant aroma emanates.
3. Add all the vegetables and the tamarind juice. Bring to the boil.
4. Add the broken wheat and pigeon peas (along with the water in which they were soaked in), turmeric powder, and salt as desired.
5. Close the pressure cooker with the lid. Remove after 3 whistles.
6. Meanwhile, heat the ghee in a small pan; fry the cashews until golden.
7. Garnish the bisibelebhath with coriander leaves and cashews. Serve hot.

Bisibelebhath Powder Mix

1 tsp split black gram (dhuli urad dal)
1 tsp split Bengal gram (dhuli chana dal)
1 tbsp fenugreek seeds*
3–4 red chillies
2 tbsp coriander seeds
4 tbsp desiccated coconut (*copra* powder)

METHOD
Add about ½ tsp oil in a pan and first roast both the dals together until brown. Add the fenugreek seeds and fry till red. Add the chillies and fry for about a minute. Then add the coriander seeds and fry all together till the raw smell of the coriander goes. Finally, add the coconut and fry together for a minute and let it cool. Then powder it in a mixer. This powder can be used in step 5.

Karnataka Puliyodhara

● ●

INGREDIENTS
2 cups rice, washed
1 lemon-sized ball tamarind*, soaked in ½ cup water for 10 minutes
¼ tsp fenugreek seeds*
1 tbsp coriander seeds*
6 red chillies
½ tsp cumin* seeds
¼ tsp black peppercorns
5 tsp groundnut oil / gingelly oil*
2 tbsp jaggery*
1 tsp mustard seeds
½ tbsp split black gram, skinless (dhuli urad dal)*
½ tbsp split Bengal gram (chana dal)*
3 tbsp groundnuts, broken
15–20 curry leaves
½ tsp sesame seeds
½ desiccated coconut (copra powder)
Salt to taste

- *The paste prepared in step 4 can be had as a side, along with curd rice or chapattis.**
- *This dish stays fresh and flavourful in any temperature. In southern India, this dish is commonly wrapped in banana leaves and packed for travel meals.*
- *You can also powder some roasted cashews and sesame seeds and add to the rice in the end before serving.*

METHOD

1. Put the rice in a cooker. Add 2–2½ cups water and cook until 4 whistles. Remove from heat and allow the pressure to be fully released. Open the lid and allow the rice to cool. After a few minutes, transfer the rice to a large open vessel. Mix a bit of salt in it and set aside. (The rice grains should be soft, but should not stick to each other.)

2. Extract the tamarind juice and set aside.

3. Place the fenugreek seeds in a thick-bottomed pan and roast until fragrant. Add the coriander seeds, 4 red chillies, cumin seeds, and peppercorns. Roast lightly and remove from heat. Cool and grind into powder.

4. Heat 4 tsp oil in another pan; add the mustard seeds and as they begin to splutter, add the black gram, Bengal gram, and 2 red chillies. Lightly crush the groundnuts and add. Sauté until the groundnuts turn golden brown in colour. (Ensure the groundnuts are evenly browned. They are a key component in the final texture and flavour of the dish.)

5. Add the curry leaves and the tamarind juice and allow it to boil until the raw smell of tamarind disappears.

6. Add the ground powder (step 3) to the tamarind mix.

7. Heat the remaining oil in a pan and add the sesame seeds. As they begin to crackle, add it to the tamarind mix. In the same pan, roast the grated coconut until fragrant. Remove from heat and add to the mix.

8. Add the mix in small quantities to the rice until it suits your taste. Mix well. (If desired, add a drizzle of hot gingelly or sesame oil so the paste mixes well with the rice.)

9. Serve hot or at room temperature with a potato dish, chips or curd.

Pranic Foods

Sadhguru

WHAT ARE PRANIC FOODS?

In Yoga, we do not look at food in terms of proteins, vitamins and minerals. Instead, it is categorized in terms of positive pranic, negative pranic and zero pranic. Positive pranic foods are those substances which, when consumed, add *prana* (life energy) to the system. Negative pranic foods take away prana from the system. Zero pranic foods neither add nor take away prana; they are just eaten for taste.

NEGATIVE PRANIC FOODS

The negative pranic foods are garlic, onion, asafoetida, chilli,[2] brinjal (eggplant), coffee, tea, alcohol and all nervous stimulants and intoxicants. Some substances hype the nervous system, some put it down – anything that plays upon the nervous system is negative pranic. Everything else can be consumed except these items.

In India, we say all these negative pranic substances were created by Sage Vishwamitra.

One day, he got into a tiff with God. He wanted to push his own people into heaven. God said, 'No, your people cannot come.'

He got wild with anger and said, 'Then I am going to make my own creation.'

---

[2] In the Isha Yoga Centre, red chilli is used in moderation for taste. However, in all the recipes mentioned here, chilli can be omitted or replaced with black pepper for a completely positive pranic adaptation.

So Vishwamitra made his own private earth, his own hell, and his own heaven for his people. He tried to push his favourite disciple, Trishanku, to heaven. Trishanku went up half the way and got stuck there. He could neither go forward nor backward. Even now in India if you say 'Trishanku', it means you are in limbo. You can neither go here nor there. You are stuck in between.

The point of this story is that if you consume these negative pranic substances, you become emotionally unstable, and in turn, you will be in a limbo all your life. Whatever you do – whether you are living in a family, running a business, pursuing academics or spirituality, it doesn't matter – your full potential will never be made use of. Vishwamitra is a symbol of this.

When you are running a business, you don't have to get angry twenty-four hours of the day. Even if you get angry with one client or one customer every day, it is enough to ruin your business. If you are married, and you get angry with your partner for just five minutes every day, it is enough to mess up your marriage. To avoid the emotional instability which could land one in such situations, one would be wise to stay away from negative pranic foods.

You can consume these foods of course, but they are habit-forming. If you consume these foods for a certain period of time, after that you have no choice – they compel you.

Garlic and Onion

Garlic is a powerful medicine if properly used, but consuming it as a day-to-day food stuff is a completely different issue. If you want to know what kind of damage garlic causes, make an ounce of garlic juice and drink it on an empty stomach. You will have to be taken to a hospital for a stomach wash. That's the kind of reaction it will produce. The same will happen if you drink an ounce of onion juice, but with onion, even as you are cutting it, your body is saying 'no.' But you won't leave it because someone has told you it is good for you. Suppose you are told that if you eat one clove of garlic, you will fall dead; you wouldn't even consider eating it. Or if it was bitter, you would not eat it. The problem is that it tastes good and the damage happens slowly, over a period of time.

Chilli

Another negative pranic food is chilli (green or red). In India, there is no meal without chilli. For people from other countries who visit India, their biggest threat is Indian curry. People who are not used to chilli just cannot hold it in their stomach. They will have diarrhoea, which means the body is treating the chilli almost like poison. It wants to purge. Even if you have been used to eating chilli for a long time, go off it for just thirty days, and then take in a little. Immediately, you will have diarrhoea.

You need to understand that the body has a tremendous ability to adapt to whatever you give it. If you start eating mud every day, slowly the system will adapt itself to manage that as well. But that does not make it the ideal food.

Brinjal

Brinjal (eggplant) is the only vegetable which has a certain poison in it and tends to cause damage to the brain. It is not that if you eat one brinjal your brain will cease to work. The damage will happen over a period of time. For five years if you eat brinjal every day, I assure you, you will be a much duller person than what you are right now. If you have growing children in your house, brinjal should be banished because it will sabotage their intelligence before they grow up.

Coffee

If you drink coffee for five days, on the sixth day the coffee commands you – drink! After that, there is no choice.

Coffee is a very powerful stimulant. In the morning, just with two sips of coffee everything becomes bright and clear. It makes you feel superhuman all of a sudden. But if you drink it every day, after some time you will see that when you drink a cup of coffee, two hours later you will get a headache. You have to drink another cup of coffee to fix that.

Experiment and see. Go off coffee for two months, then drink a strong cup of coffee early in the morning. You will find that your hands tremble. That means it is definitely causing some harm to the system. Does it mean you should give up coffee? That is your choice. I will not ask you to give up this or that. All I am telling you is: don't live like a slave to anything, whatever that damn thing is. Learn to live consciously. Whether it is coffee, or a cigarette, or God, learn to live consciously with all those aspects. You do what you want as long as it is happening by choice. Once it starts becoming a compulsion, then it is a problem. Anything that becomes a compulsion naturally becomes ugly.

Only you can judge how much of what to bring into your life, but if you abuse stimulants, there will be a price to pay. If you consume nervous stimulants, your old age can be misery. If the attitude is 'After all, our life is short. Instead of living to ninety, if I live to seventy, what the hell!', it is fine. I'm not against it nor am I against coffee. I also enjoy coffee, but it is not something that I do compulsively. If you like the taste of it, then drink it – drink the largest cup and thoroughly enjoy it. But if the attitude is 'I must do it every day', then there is a problem.

ZERO PRANIC FOODS

There are a few foods which are zero pranic, like potatoes and tomatoes. They can be consumed by healthy adults, but people who have swelling and aching joints should avoid them. They tend to aggravate joint problems like rheumatism or arthritis. Even if you have no specific ailment but your legs tend to get swollen, it is best to avoid these two foods.

Zero pranic substances increase your sleep quota because they bring inertia to the system. That is why we usually discourage students and meditators from consuming them. For students, a textbook is always such a great tranquillizer. The moment they open it, they fall asleep. And for a meditator, for someone who wants to sit with eyes closed and be fully alert, the biggest enemy is sleep. So, for such people, consumption of potatoes and tomatoes should be reduced.

POSITIVE PRANIC FOODS

Everything other than the zero pranic and negative pranic foods – all other vegetables, nuts, sprouts, fruits and dry fruits – are positive pranic.

Curries and Subzis

Find both exotic recipes like the Banana Flower Dal Fry and classic recipes like Palak (Spinach) *Subzi* in this section. These vegetable side dishes are perfect complements to rice, *chapatti* and other main cereals or grain dishes.

Agathi Leaves Fry

....

This dish is traditionally eaten on *Dwadashi* (the day after *Ekadashi* when many people fast). As *agathi* helps the stomach in digestion, it is served the day after the fast to soothe the stomach from gas and other ailments.

Agathi Leaves with Coconut

INGREDIENTS
2 bunches agathi leaves*, leaves separated from stem, washed well
1 tsp turmeric powder*
3 tsp oil
¼ tsp fenugreek seeds*
½ tsp mustard seeds
½ tsp split black gram, skinless (dhuli urad dal)*
1 red chilli
2"-piece coconut, fresh, grated
Salt to taste

- *This dish can be had mixed with ghee and rice or as a side to a larger meal. Cooked split pigeon peas (dhuli toovar dal)* can also be added before serving.*
- *To separate the agathi leaves from stem, hold the stem between the thumb and index finger and slide down, easily removing the leaves.*
- *If desired, add coconut milk* and eat it as a soup, or pour it on rice for a rich tasting gravy.*

71

METHOD

1. Boil the agathi leaves in water with a pinch of turmeric and salt. Drain the water. (This water can be reserved and consumed, either as drinking water, or added into sambar* or *rasam*. It is said to be healing for the stomach, and carries the medicinal properties of agathi.)
2. Place the leaves in a pan with a little salt and cook until soft.
3. In another pan, heat the oil and add the mustard seeds, fenugreek seeds, and split black gram.
4. As they begin to change colour, add the red chilli and coconut.
5. Add this tempering to the agathi leaves.
6. Mix and remove from heat. Serve.

Agathi Leaves — Sweet and Salty

INGREDIENTS
2 bunches agathi leaves*, leaves separated from stem, washed well
1 tsp rice
1 red chilli
4–6 black peppercorns
1 tsp split Bengal gram (dhuli chana dal)*
1 jaggery* piece, marble-sized, crushed
Salt to taste

METHOD
1. Heat a small pan. One by one roast the rice, red chilli, black peppercorns and split Bengal gram. Keep aside to cool.
2. When cool, put the mixture into a blender and grind to a coarse powder.
3. Place the agathi leaves in a pan with a little salt and cook until soft.
4. Add the jaggery and sprinkle the roasted rice and spice powder. Mix well.
5. Adjust salt and mix. Serve. If desired, grated coconut can be added before serving.

> • *This dish can be had mixed with ghee and rice, or as a side to a larger meal. Cooked split pigeon peas (dhuli toovar dal)* can also be added before serving.*

Banana Flower Dal Fry

INGREDIENTS

1 banana flower*, trimmed, chopped *(See tip)*
½ cup split pigeon peas (dhuli toovar dal)*, washed, soaked in 2 cups water for 1 hour
¼ cup split Bengal gram (dhuli chana dal)*, soaked in 2 cups water for 1 hour
2 red chillies
2 tsp oil
½ tsp mustard seeds
½ tsp split black gram, skinless (dhuli urad dal)*
7–8 curry leaves
¼ cup coconut, fresh, grated
Salt to taste

METHOD

1. Drain the water and put the dals in a mixer with the red chillies and salt, and grind into a coarse paste using only a little water, if required.

- *Wash the banana flower with water. Apply oil on your hands so the sap of the flower does not stick to your hands and clothing and remove the red petals from the banana flower. Collect all the blossoms inside. Open them and remove the hard stamen and plastic-like petal. Cut off the stems. The innermost cone part of the flower can also be chopped and used. To prevent discolouration, keep in a bowl of buttermilk with a pinch of turmeric, until ready to use.*

74

2. Steam the banana flower in a pan until soft.
3. Heat the oil in another pan; add the mustard seeds. As they begin to splutter, add the black gram and curry leaves.
4. Add the dal paste and sauté on medium-low heat until the mixture begins to leave the sides of the pan.
5. Add the cooked banana flower to it and continue to sauté for 1–2 minutes.
6. Adjust the salt and add the coconut. Mix everything well together and remove the pan from the heat. Serve.

Broccoli Fry

• •

INGREDIENTS
1 broccoli, medium-sized head, separated into small florets, cut into small even-sized pieces
1 tbsp sunflower oil / olive oil
4–5 curry leaves, fresh
¼ tsp fenugreek seeds*
1 tsp cumin* seeds
1½ tsp *garam masala* powder* (optional)
¾–1 tsp black pepper powder
1 tbsp lemon juice
Salt to taste

METHOD
1. Heat oil in the pan; add the curry leaves, fenugreek seeds, and cumin seeds. As they begin to change colour, add the garam masala powder, followed by broccoli. Sauté well. (If desired, add a little chopped tomato before adding broccoli. As the tomato cooks, it will make for a rich and spicy gravy. Alternatively, mango powder can also be added in this step.)

• *Broccoli stems are highly nutritious and can be chopped and included into this dish.*
• *Broccoli cooks very fast and is tastier when it has a bite to it. To prevent overcooking of broccoli (and loss of nutrients), remove the broccoli from the pan when it is still vibrant green in colour.*

76

2. Sprinkle a little water. Add salt to taste. Stir for about 3-5 minutes.
3. Once the broccoli is soft, add pepper powder and cook for half a minute.
4. Remove the pan from the heat. Add the lemon juice and stir.
5. This can be served with rice, rolled into chapatti* or sandwiched between two buttered toasts.

Amaranth Fry

••

INGREDIENTS
1 bunch amaranth leaves*, washed, drained, finely chopped into ribbons
2 tsp oil
½ tsp mustard seeds
1 tsp split black gram, skinless (dhuli urad dal)*
1 tsp cumin* seeds
3 red chillies
½ tbsp sambar powder*
2"-piece coconut, fresh, grated
10–12 curry leaves
Salt to taste

METHOD
1. Heat the oil in a broad pan; add the mustard seeds and as they begin to splutter add the black gram, cumin seeds, and red chillies.
2. Add the sambar powder and amaranth leaves; sauté for 1–2 minutes. Cover the pan and cook on medium-low flame. Open the lid after 2 minutes and add salt. Stir well and cook, covered, stirring occasionally.
3. Once cooked, add the coconut along with the curry leaves. Mix well. Remove from heat.
4. Serve garnished with roasted groundnuts or almond slivers, if desired.

• *Amaranth can be substituted by any green, leafy vegetable.*
• *This can also be made with the addition of cooked skinless split green gram (dhuli moong dal).* Simply add the gram in step 3 along with the amaranth leaves.*

Beans Dal Fry

• •

INGREDIENTS
15-20 French beans, stringed, washed, chopped into small pieces
½ cup split Bengal gram (dhuli chana dal)*, washed, soaked in 2 cups water for ½ hour
½ cup split pigeon peas (dhuli toovar dal)*, washed, soaked in 2 cups water for ½ hour
4 tsp oil
1 tsp mustard seeds
10-12 curry leaves
6 red chillies
Salt to taste

METHOD
1. Heat a little oil in a pan; add the beans and cook well, adding salt to taste.
2. Drain the water from the dals. Then put the dals, 3 red chillies and a few curry leaves in a blender with salt; grind to a coarse paste. (If needed, add a little water to maintain the paste-like consistency.)
3. Heat the oil in a pan; add the mustard seeds. As they begin to splutter, add the remaining curry leaves, red chillies, and dal paste. Cook until the paste begins to leave the sides of the pan.
4. Add the cooked beans and salt to taste; sauté well.
5. Serve.

Aviyal (Mixed Vegetables)

. . . .

INGREDIENTS
6" slice ash gourd*, peeled, chopped into 2"-long pieces
1 plantain*, peeled, chopped into 2"-long pieces
10–12 French beans, stringed, chopped
1 drumstick*, chopped into 2"-long pieces
2 carrots, medium-sized, peeled, cut into 2"-long pieces
1 elephant yam*, small, peeled, chopped into 2"-long pieces
½ coconut, fresh, chopped into pieces
1 tsp cumin* seeds
2 red chillies
2 tbsp coconut oil
8–10 curry leaves
1 cup curd
Turmeric powder* to taste
Salt to taste

- *Just about any vegetable can be added to aviyal (beetroot, however, tends to discolour the dish). Raw mango is often cooked and added for a sour and tangy taste. In this case, curd can be reduced or omitted.*
- *Instead of boiling the vegetables, one can also steam for about 10 minutes or until soft.*
- *If desired, tamarind* water can be substituted for curd.*
- *Coconut oil gives the aviyal its aroma and taste, so it is best not to substitute with any other oil.*

METHOD

1. Boil the ash gourd, plantain, beans, drumstick, and carrots in water along with turmeric powder and salt. Cook until the vegetables are soft. Drain the water and keep the vegetables aside. (This water can be added to the *aviyal* later to adjust the consistency.)

2. Put the elephant yam in a pan and pour just enough water to cover. Sprinkle salt and cook on low heat until soft. (Any other additional vegetable that takes longer to cook should be cooked separately.)

2. Put the coconut into a blender. Add the cumin seeds and red chillies and grind to a coarse paste.

4. Place the yam and boiled vegetables in a deep serving bowl and add the ground paste, coconut oil, curry leaves, and curd. Mix lightly. (Aviyal can be served with a lot of gravy or as a thick curry. Adjust the amount of curd and vegetable water.)

5. Serve along with rice, *appams* or even as a stew.

Ridge Gourd Koottu

INGREDIENTS

3 ridge gourds*, peeled, chopped
¼ cup split green gram, skinless (dhuli moong dal)*, washed, soaked in 1 cup water for 30 minutes
¼ cup split Bengal gram (dhuli chana dal)*, washed, soaked in 1 cup water for 30 minutes
3"-piece coconut, fresh, grated
1 tsp cumin* seeds
5 red chillies
2 tbsp coconut oil
1 tsp mustard seeds
10–12 curry leaves
3 tomatoes, small, chopped
Salt to taste

METHOD

1. Drain and cook each dal separately in a pressure cooker till one whistle. Keep aside. (Each dal will need ½ cup of fresh water. Ensure that the dals are not too soft or the dish will become more like gravy.)
2. Put the coconut, cumin seeds, and red chillies in a blender. Use a little water and make a paste. Keep aside.
3. Heat the oil in a pan; add the mustard seeds. As they begin to splutter, add most of the curry leaves.

4. Add the tomatoes and sauté until the oil comes to the surface.
5. Add the ridge gourds and stir well.
6. Dissolve the coconut paste in a little water and add to the ridge gourd mixture. Add the salt and bring to boil.
7. Add the boiled Bengal gram and stir lightly.
8. Add the boiled green gram and stir lightly.
9. Add the remaining curry leaves; mix well. Remove the pan from heat.
10. Serve.

Snake Gourd Koottu

•••

INGREDIENTS

500 g snake gourd*, cut into small pieces
½ cup split green gram, skinless (dhuli moong dal)*, washed,
soaked in 1 cup water for 30 minutes
2 tsp coconut oil
1 tsp split black gram, skinless (dhuli urad dal)*
3 red chillies
6–8 black peppercorns
1 tsp cumin* seeds
½ coconut, fresh, grated
4–5 sprigs coriander leaves*, fresh, chopped
10–12 curry leaves
½ tsp mustard seeds
Salt to taste

METHOD

1. Drain and cook the green gram in 2 cups of fresh water, until three-fourths done.
2. Add the snake gourd with salt to taste. Continue to cook on low heat until fully done.
3. Meanwhile, heat 1 tsp coconut oil in a pan. Add ½ tsp black gram, red chillies, and black peppercorns. Sauté until the black gram turns golden brown in colour.
4. Add the cumin seeds and sauté for a few seconds.

5. Add the coconut and mix well; remove from heat. Cool and grind to a paste.

6. Add this coconut paste to the cooked snake gourd and bring to boil.

7. Add the coriander leaves along with half of the curry leaves. Mix.

8. Heat the remaining coconut oil in a small pan; add the mustard seeds. As they begin to splutter, add the remaining ½ tsp black gram and the remaining curry leaves.

9. Pour this seasoning on the *koottu*. Mix well.

10. Serve.

Stuffed Okra

• •

INGREDIENTS
500 g okras*, washed, wiped dry, top and tail trimmed, slit
lengthwise with ends joined
¼ cup groundnuts
1"-piece ginger, peeled, finely grated
¼ cup gram flour*
1½ tsp garam masala powder*
1 tbsp jaggery*, crumbled
2 tsp lemon juice
Oil for frying
Salt to taste

METHOD
1. Put the groundnuts in a pan and roast until fragrant and lightly
   brown. When cool, remove the skin. Place in the mixer and
   grind coarsely.
2. Add the ginger to the groundnut powder along with the gram
   flour, garam masala powder, salt to taste, crumbled jaggery,
   and lemon juice. Mix well. Stuff a little bit of this mixture into
   each okra so that all the cut surfaces are well covered.
3. Heat the oil in a wok *(kadhai)*; fry the stuffed okras until crisp.
   Remove with a slotted spoon and drain the excess oil on
   absorbent kitchen towels.
4. Serve hot.

• *Wipe the okras well, otherwise they will become sticky while
  cooking. It is best to select small and tender okras for this
  recipe. If the tip breaks easily, the okra is tender.*
• *If desired, coconut can also be added to the paste.*

Okra Masala

• •

INGREDIENTS

500 g okras*, tender, washed, wiped, dried, top and tail trimmed
4 tomatoes, medium-sized
3 tbsp butter
1 tbsp ginger paste
2 tsp cumin* powder
1 tsp turmeric powder*
1 tsp red chilli powder
10 cashews, soaked in 1 cup of water for 30 minutes, ground to a paste
¼ coconut, fresh, grated, ground to a paste using ¼ cup of water
Oil for frying
Salt to taste

METHOD

1. Place the tomatoes in a pan and pour just enough water to cover. Boil for 1–2 minutes and then remove the pan from the heat. Drain the water. Cool the tomatoes and remove the skin. Chop them roughly and grind to a paste.
2. Heat sufficient oil in a wok (kadhai); fry the okras until crisp. Remove with a slotted spoon and drain the excess oil on absorbent kitchen towels.
3. Heat the butter on low heat; add the ginger paste and sauté for 1 minute.
4. Add the tomato paste and sauté for 1 minute.
5. Add the cumin powder, turmeric powder, and red chilli powder. Sauté for 1 minute.
6. Add the cashew nut paste and sauté for 2 minutes.
7. Add the coconut paste and sauté until the fat separates.
8. Add the fried okras and salt; mix well.
9. Remove the wok from heat.
10. Serve hot.

Karnataka Vegetable Subzi

• •

INGREDIENTS

400 g cauliflower, soaked in hot water for 10 minutes, drained, chopped into small pieces
3 tomatoes, medium-sized, chopped into small pieces
150 g green peas
4 tsp oil
½ tsp mustard seeds
2 tbsp split Bengal gram (dhuli chana dal)*
2 tbsp split black gram, skinless (dhuli urad dal)*
½ tbsp coriander seeds*
1 tsp cumin* seeds
3 red chillies
1" stick cinnamon*
3 cloves*
3 green cardamom* pods
Salt to taste

METHOD

1. Put the Bengal gram, black gram, coriander seeds, cumin seeds, red chillies, cinnamon, cloves, and cardamom pods in a pan and roast until they turn golden brown in colour. Cool and grind to a powder.
2. Heat the oil in a pan; add the mustard seeds. As they begin to splutter, add the cauliflower, tomatoes, green peas, and salt. Sauté for 2–3 minutes.
3. Add ¼ cup of water, mix well. Cook, covered with a lid, stirring occasionally.
4. Once the cauliflower is cooked, add the prepared powder and stir well. Cook, on low heat, for 1–2 minutes. Mix and serve.

Palak (Spinach) Subzi

INGREDIENTS

3 bunches spinach leaves (palak), fresh, cleaned, roots removed, leaves and stems washed, drained, chopped
¼ cup cashews, soaked in ¼ cup water for 30 minutes
2 tbsp ghee*
½ tsp cumin* seeds
1½ tsp garam masala powder*
1½ tsp cumin* powder
1 tbsp coriander powder*
1½ tsp red chilli powder
Salt to taste

METHOD

1. Cook the spinach, covered, on low heat until soft. Cool and grind to a paste.
2. Drain and grind the cashews to a paste.
3. Heat the ghee in a pan; add the cumin seeds, garam masala powder, cumin powder, coriander powder, and red chilli powder. Stir.
4. Add the cashew nut paste and sauté until the fat separates.
5. Add the spinach paste and salt to taste; sauté for 2-3 minutes.
6. Serve.

- *This is an excellent side dish with chapatti*, roti, and naan. Fried cottage cheese or boiled potato added to this subzi enhances the taste and creates a more substantial texture.*

Groundnut Capsicum Subzi

••

INGREDIENTS

½ cup groundnuts
3 capsicums, medium-sized, halved, deseeded, chopped into
small even-sized pieces
3 tsp oil
½ tsp cumin* seeds
1 tsp white sesame seeds
½ cup gram flour*
1½ tsp sugar
Salt to taste

METHOD

1. Put the groundnuts in a pan and roast until fragrant and lightly
   brown. When cool, remove the skin. Place in the mixer and
   grind coarsely.
2. Heat 2 tsp oil in a pan; add the cumin seeds. As they begin to
   change colour, add the sesame seeds and groundnut powder.
   Stir well.
3. Add the capsicum and salt to taste; mix well. Cook on low heat
   until done.
4. Meanwhile, heat the remaining oil in another pan. Add the
   gram flour and sauté, on low heat, until the gram flour becomes
   fragrant and turns golden brown in colour.
5. Add the sugar and mix. Sauté for 5–7 minutes on low heat.
6. Add the cooked capsicum and mix well. Adjust the salt; sauté
   for 1 minute. Remove from heat and serve.

The Endless Debate
Veg or Non-veg?

Sadhguru

ASK YOUR BODY

Vegetarians always act 'holier than thou', while non-vegetarians always claim they are more robust and fit for the world, as they treat all species on the planet as part of their menu. Many philosophies have evolved based on the choice of food. But one must remember there is nothing religious, philosophical, spiritual or moral about the food one eats. It is only a question of whether the food is compatible with the kind of body one has.

This compatibility can be towards various ends. If you just want to grow like a bull, if being big is your highest aspiration, then certain types of foods have to be consumed. If you want a body that supports a high level of intelligence, or a body with a certain level of alertness, awareness and agility, other types of foods must be consumed. If you want a body that is highly perceptive – if you are not someone who will settle just for health and pleasure, but want to download the cosmos – you will need to eat in a very different way. For every aspiration that a human being has, he will have to manage his food accordingly; or if your aspirations involve all these dimensions, you will have to find a suitable balance.

If it is just a question of basic survival, eat whatever you want. But once survival is taken care of and there is a choice about what to eat, it is very important that this choice becomes conscious – not simply led by the compulsion of the tongue but by the essential design of one's body. If you listen to your body, your body will clearly tell you what kind of food it is happy with. But right now, you are listening to your mind. Your mind keeps lying to you all the time. Hasn't it lied to you before? Today it tells you 'this is it!' Tomorrow it makes you feel like a fool for what you believed yesterday. So don't go by your mind. You just have to learn to listen to your body. It takes a certain mindfulness and attention to do this. Once you have that, you will know what to eat and what not to eat.

INTEGRATING A SIMPLE SOFTWARE

In terms of the quality of food entering you, vegetarian food is definitely far better for the system than non-vegetarian. We are not looking at it from a moral standpoint. We are looking at what is suitable for the system and is comfortable for the body.

When you eat food, you are taking another life – either plant or animal – and making it your life. Essentially, all life on the planet is coming from the earth. Whether it is a human being or an earthworm, it is the same soil. But if I eat a mango, the mango becomes a man in me. If a cow eats a mango, the same mango becomes a cow. This is happening because there is a certain information or, in modern terminology, a software in you that transforms what you eat into a man or a woman. Every life is happening the way it is happening because of a certain dimension of information.

The idea is to eat that kind of life which is a very simple software. Then your ability to override that software and make it entirely a part of you is good. It is from this context that it is important to eat a vegetarian diet. As the software gets more complex, your ability to integrate it goes down. Especially if it is a creature that has some sense of thought and emotion, it will not integrate, and that animal nature will start manifesting itself in you. In other words, we are incapable of complete integration of the more evolved, intelligent and emotionally

93

endowed creatures. You may get nourishment, but that software does not break down as completely as it would with that of a vegetable or a fruit.

DOES VEGETARIAN FOOD GIVE YOU ENOUGH NUTRITION?

The problem with today's vegetarian meal is that it is so overcooked that most of the nutrients are destroyed. If at least 50-60 per cent of your food is uncooked vegetarian material, your system will be in its best health. Also, because of the way crops are grown today, their nutritional quality is compromised. If you eat what is grown on the farm today, you are bound to get B-12 deficiencies and other kinds of problems. If you consume organically grown food, this will not be an issue.

Some people think that a vegetarian diet will make you develop protein deficiencies or anaemia. No. It is just that in your vegetarian diet, you may be eating only certain types of foods. Anaemic conditions may occur because you tend to eat only salads and fruits. If you eat sufficient amount of nuts, lentils, sprouted grams, some amount of cereal and honey, you will have a full diet. Your protein requirement will also be taken care of.

One aspect of vegetarian diet is that you have to be conscious about what you eat; you have to ensure you are eating a variety of foods. With non-vegetarian food you don't have to worry, you just eat a piece of meat and the basic nourishment is taken care of – in a gross way, but it is taken care of. You won't have these kinds of deficiency problems at least. Vegetarian diet needs much more awareness to consume. The very process of eating vegetarian food demands a certain level of attention and also leads to a heightened level of awareness. But people don't have that kind of involvement in what they consume and want to just pop in something and be okay. So, naturally, they have shifted to non-vegetarian diet in a big way.

Kuzhambus

Kuzhambu refers to a gravy that accompanies the main carbohydrate dish of a meal, usually rice or a kali made from a particular cereal. A must in most southern Indian meals. Here are a few well-known traditional kuzhambus from Tamil Nadu.

Sodhi

••

INGREDIENTS
1 coconut, fresh, grated
1 drumstick*, trimmed, cut into finger-length pieces
1 potato, medium-sized, peeled, chopped into small even-sized pieces
2 tomatoes, medium-sized, chopped
2 tsp ginger, peeled, finely grated
1 tsp coriander powder*
½ tsp turmeric powder*
1 tsp red chilli powder
2 tsp coconut oil
½ tsp mustard seeds
8–10 curry leaves
4–5 sprigs coriander leaves*, fresh
Salt to taste

METHOD
1. Place the coconut in the mixer. Add 2 cups of water and grind to a smooth paste. Strain through a thick, clean cloth and extract the 'first' thick milk.
2. Put the coconut residue in the mixer again and pour 2 cups of water. Grind again to a smooth paste. Strain through a thick, clean cloth and extract the 'second' thin milk.

- *This dish can be served along with rice noodles and string hoppers.*

3. Boil the potato for 3–5 minutes and set aside.
4. Pour the thin coconut milk in a pan. Add the drumstick, potato, tomatoes, ginger, turmeric powder, coriander powder, and red chilli powder. Cook on low heat until the vegetables are cooked. Remove the pan from the heat.
5. Add the thick coconut milk and salt to taste. Stir well.
6. Heat the oil in another pan; add the mustard seeds. As they begin to splutter, add the curry leaves.
7. Pour the tempering on the *sodhi*. Add the coriander leaves; mix and serve.

Banana Stem Sambar

• •

INGREDIENTS
6"-piece banana stem*, fibrous parts removed, cut into round pieces
1 cup split pigeon peas (dhuli toovar dal)*, washed, soaked
2 tsp oil
1½ tsp coriander seeds*
¾ tsp split black gram, skinless (dhuli urad dal)*
1 tsp split Bengal gram (dhuli chana dal)*
½ tsp fenugreek seeds*
5 red chillies
½ cup coconut, fresh, grated
1 tamarind*, lemon-sized piece, soaked in 1 cup water, juice extracted
1 tbsp jaggery*
½ tsp turmeric powder*
½ tsp mustard seeds
7–8 curry leaves
4–5 sprigs coriander leaves*, fresh, chopped
Salt to taste

METHOD
1. Place the pigeon peas in a pan with the turmeric powder and 2 cups of water, and cook until done. Keep aside.
2. Heat 1 tsp oil in a pan; lightly roast the coriander seeds, black gram, Bengal gram, fenugreek seeds, and red chillies.

3. Add the coconut and sauté until the coconut is lightly coloured. Remove from heat. Cool and grind.
4. Mix the tamarind juice, jaggery, and a little salt with the banana stem and cook with 1 cup of water until soft.
5. Add the ground paste to the cooked banana stem. To this, add the cooked pigeon peas and boil it well.
6. Heat the remaining 1 tsp oil in a pan and add the mustard seeds. As they begin to splutter, add the curry leaves.
7. Add the tempering to the banana stem preparation and mix well. Remove from heat.
8. Serve garnished with coriander leaves.

Fenugreek Kuzhambu

. . . .

INGREDIENTS
1 tsp fenugreek seeds*
2 tbsp gingelly oil*
¼ tsp mustard seeds
½ tsp split black gram, skinless (dhuli urad dal)*
½ tsp split Bengal gram (dhuli chana dal)*
2 red chillies
¼ tsp cumin* seeds
8–10 curry leaves
1 tamarind*, lemon-sized ball, soaked in 1 cup water, thick juice extracted
2 tsp sambar powder*
½ tsp turmeric powder*
Salt to taste

METHOD
1. Heat 1 tbsp oil in a pan. Add the mustard seeds. As they begin to splutter, add the fenugreek seeds, black gram, Bengal gram, red chillies, cumin seeds, and curry leaves.
2. Add the tamarind juice.
3. Add the sambar powder, salt, and turmeric powder; stir well.
4. Allow the seasoning and tamarind mixture to come to boil and cook until it reduces to half its original amount.
5. Remove the pan from heat and add the remaining oil.
6. Mix well and serve.

Ginger and Coconut Kadhi

••

INGREDIENTS
1 cup curd
50 g ginger, washed, peeled, finely chopped
½ coconut, fresh, grated
2 tsp coconut oil
½ tsp fenugreek seeds*
10–12 curry leaves
½ tsp red chilli powder
½ tsp mustard seeds
½ tsp split black gram, skinless (dhuli urad dal)*
1 dried red chilli
Salt to taste

METHOD
1. Heat 1 tsp oil in a small pan; fry the fenugreek seeds and curry leaves. Keep aside.
2. Put the ginger, coconut, fried fenugreek seeds and curry leaves with the red chilli powder in a mixer and grind to a smooth paste.
3. Heat the remaining oil in a pan; add the mustard seeds. As they begin to splutter, add the dal and the dried red chilli.
4. Add the ginger-coconut paste. Add ¼ cup of water, mix and cook, on low heat, for a few minutes. Remove from heat.
5. Add the curd and salt to taste. Mix well and serve.

Kadhi (Moar Kuzhambu)

....

INGREDIENTS
½ cup gram flour*
2 cups curd
2 tsp ghee*
½ tsp fenugreek seeds*
1"-stick cinnamon*
3 cloves*
3 red chillies
10–12 curry leaves
¼ tsp turmeric powder*
¼ tsp garam masala powder*
Salt to taste

METHOD
1. Place the gram flour with the curd in a deep vessel and mix thoroughly.
2. Add 5 cups of water and mix well.
3. Heat the ghee in a pan; add the fenugreek seeds, cinnamon, cloves, red chillies, curry leaves, and turmeric powder; sauté for half a minute.
4. Add the gram flour-curd mixture, stir and allow it to come to boil.
5. Once it boils, add the salt and garam masala powder. After 5 minutes, remove the pan from heat.
6. Serve hot.

Pakoda Kuzhambu

....

INGREDIENTS
1 cup split Bengal gram (dhuli chana dal)*, soaked in 3 cups of
water for 2 hours, drained
1½"-piece ginger, peeled, chopped
3 red chillies
1 tsp fennel seeds*
1 carrot, small, peeled, grated
1 tbsp ghee*
7-8 curry leaves
7-8 sprigs coriander leaves*, fresh, finely chopped
4 tomatoes, medium-sized
1" stick cinnamon*
1 bay leaf
3-4 cloves*
2 tsp coriander powder*
½ tsp turmeric powder*
2 cups coconut milk*
3 tbsp cashew nut paste
1 tbsp red chilli powder
Oil for frying + 3 tbsp oil for tempering
Salt to taste

| • *This can be served with rice or chapatti*.

METHOD

1. Put the Bengal gram in a mixer with the ginger, red chillies, and fennel seeds, and grind to a coarse paste. Add salt to taste, carrot, melted ghee, curry leaves and half of the chopped coriander leaves. Mix well. Divide the mixture equally into small portions and shape each into a ball.
2. Heat sufficient oil in a wok (kadhai); fry the *pakodas* until golden brown in colour. Remove with a slotted spoon and drain the excess oil on absorbent kitchen towels. Keep aside.
3. Place the tomatoes in a pan and pour just enough water to cover. Boil for 1-2 minutes and remove the pan from the heat. Drain the water. Cool the tomatoes and remove the skin. Chop them roughly and grind to a paste.
4. Heat 3 tbsp oil in a pan; add the cinnamon, bay leaf, and cloves; sauté for half a minute. Add the tomato paste, coriander powder, red chilli powder, and turmeric powder; sauté until the raw smell disappears.
5. Add the coconut milk and cook on low heat for 10 minutes. Do not allow it to come to the boil.
6. Add the cashew nut paste, mix well and cook for 5 minutes more.
7. Add salt to taste and mix. Add the pakodas back to the sauce and boil for 3 minutes. Remove the pan from the heat.
8. Sprinkle the remaining coriander leaves and serve.

Ekadashi

On the bi-monthly Ekadashi days, which fall on the eleventh day of the waxing and waning moon cycle, many volunteers at the Isha Yoga Centre consume only juice or fast for the whole day. Read on as Sadhguru explains why in the Indian tradition, people fast on Ekadashis.

Sadhguru

If you observe your body, you may notice that your system goes through a certain cycle once every 40-48 days. This is referred to as a *mandala*. In every single cycle, there are three days during which your body does not need food. If you are conscious of how your body functions, you will be aware that you can effortlessly go without food on those days. Even domestic animals, like cats and dogs, don't eat on certain days. Children also feel it, but most parents believe in forcing them to eat anyway. It is not necessary.

If you carefully observe your own system, you will notice that on certain days it does not need to eat. Forcing food on those days is not the wisest thing to do. This is not about fasting; it is a break that your body is asking for. Because people were not aware of these things, in India they fixed the Ekadashi day. On the eleventh day after the full moon and the eleventh day after the new moon, people fast for a day, to somehow make use of this cycle.

However, forcefully depriving your body of food for long periods of time is not constructive. If one wishes to fast for a certain period, it must always be supported with the right kind of practices. Your energy levels must be kept very high. If you are feeling low, and your body is struggling to keep itself up and you still don't eat just to prove something to yourself or to someone or to God, it is of no use. Forcefully denying yourself food when the body is demanding it can damage the system. But definitely giving it a break here and there is beneficial.

One can also go on a juice diet once or twice a month. You could drink warm water and honey the whole day. Or you can drink tender coconut water, but the best is ash gourd juice. If you are not able to manage with a liquid diet, you can go on a fruit diet. It is easy on your body and your digestive system will not have to process the normal type of food for one day.

Fasting like this lowers the number of cancerous cells in the body, because a cancerous cell needs almost twenty times more food than a normal cell. If you don't give food to the body, cancerous cells – present in every body – die first because they cannot survive without food.

You can dedicate your one day's food to someone who does not have food to eat. It will be very good for them and very good for you too.

Ekadashi Dinner

Here we talk about the different items that make up the meal which breaks the day-long Ekadashi fast at the Isha Yoga Centre.

Papaya Slice

• •

It is best to break the fast with fruit and other raw foods. Papaya is ideal, but you can also have fruit salads *(See 'Banana Fruit Salad' in the 'Salads' chapter).* It is also good to boost up with some green gram sprouts. *(See 'Sprouts – the Power Food' under the 'Techniques' section.)*

Amla Chutney

• •

INGREDIENTS
5-6 gooseberries *(amla)*, washed, halved, seeds removed
1 cup coconut, grated
1 sprig curry leaves
½ tsp cumin* seeds
2-4 red chillies
Salt to taste

METHOD
1. Put the gooseberries in a blender. Blend well.
2. Add the remaining ingredients and blend to a semi-coarse texture. If absolutely needed, at the very end, a little water may be added into the blender while grinding to achieve a chutney-like consistency.

Kala Chana Sundal

• •

INGREDIENTS
4 cups *kala chana**, soaked for 8 hours or overnight, drained
2 tbsp oil
2 tsp mustard seeds
2 tsp split black gram, skinless (dhuli urad dal)*
2 dry red chillies, broken
8–10 curry leaves
4 tbsp coconut, grated
4 tsp lemon juice
Salt to taste

METHOD
1. Boil the kala chana in water until soft.
2. Heat the oil in a pan on medium heat; add the mustard seeds and black gram. Stir lightly until the mustard seeds splutter and the gram is lightly browned.
3. Add the red chillies and curry leaves; stir well.
4. Add the boiled kala chana and salt; stir well and remove from heat.
5. Add the grated coconut and lemon juice. Mix well and serve.

• *A chutney can be made by grinding 2 tsp Bengal gram (dhuli chana dal)*, 1 tsp coriander seeds*, ¼ cup grated and dried coconut and 2-3 dry red chillies mixed into the sundal before serving.*

109

Cooked Vegetable (Poriyal)

INGREDIENTS

3 cups carrots, chopped
2 cups cabbage, finely shredded
1 cup green peas / green beans, cut into ½"-long pieces
2 tbsp oil
2 tsp mustard seeds
2 tsp split black gram, skinless (dhuli urad dal)*
2 dry red chillies, broken
8-10 curry leaves
4 tbsp coconut, grated
4 tsp lemon juice
Salt to taste

METHOD

1. Heat the oil in a pan on medium heat. Add the mustard seeds and black gram. Stir lightly until the mustard seeds splutter and the gram is lightly browned.
2. Add the carrot, cabbage, and peas (or beans); stir well.
3. Add the red chillies and curry leaves; stir well.
4. Remove from heat.
5. Add the grated coconut, lemon juice, and salt; mix well. Serve hot.

Rice Kanji

INGREDIENTS

1 cup rice
¼ cup green gram (moong dal)*
5 cups water
1 tsp cumin (*jeera*) seeds*
Salt to taste

METHOD

1. Heat the water in a vessel. Add the rice and green gram and allow it to boil. (It is best to 'overcook' the rice, so it is soft and easy to mash.)
2. Add the cumin seeds.
3. Keep stirring occasionally. Add the salt when the mixture is half cooked. When the mixture thickens, turn off the heat.
4. Serve the kanji as a base to the *poriyal, sundal,* and chutney.

- *White rice could be substituted with broken wheat.*
- *Coconut milk* can be added to the vessel (after step 4) for a richer taste and consistency.*

Tiffins and Chutneys

Take a look at a choice selection of light tiffin items in this section along with some accompanying flavourful chutneys. Often, the Isha Kitchen serves chutneys as an alternative to spicy pickles.

Appam (Hoppers)

● ●

INGREDIENTS

2 cups rice, washed, soaked in 8–10 cups water for a few hours
2 cups parboiled* rice, washed, soaked in 8–10 cups water for a few hours
¼ cup split black gram, skinless (dhuli urad dal)*, washed, soaked for 1–2 hours
½ cup coconut water
3 tbsp sugar
2 tsp baking soda
Salt to taste

METHOD

1. Drain and grind the rice (both raw and parboiled) and dal separately into smooth pastes. Mix them together, adding coconut water as needed for consistency.

- *Grinding the dal separately from the rice ensures that it becomes fluffy, and also helps in hastening fermentation. Coconut water helps in fermentation. If coconut water is not available, add grated coconut and blend well.*
- *Appams are traditionally made in an appam tawa, made of cast iron. A non-stick tawa can also be used, though the shape will not turn out the same. If using a regular tawa, spread the batter just as done for any dosa.*
- *If you wish to make sweet appams, you will need to add additional jaggery to the batter itself. Dissolve some jaggery in hot water and strain it to remove impurities, or use the prepared jaggery* syrup (See 'Jaggery – The Medicinal Sugar' in the 'Techniques' section). This addition will make very soft, sweet appams.*

2. Allow the batter to ferment overnight.
3. After fermentation, add salt, sugar, and baking soda. Mix well. (You can also add some coconut milk into the batter.) Ensure the batter is not too thick; otherwise the appams will not get properly cooked in the middle. The batter should be pouring consistency, thinner than *dosa* batter.
4. Heat an appam *tawa**. Pour a ladleful of batter into it and lightly swirl the pan to spread the batter to the sides of the pan. Cover with a lid and cook for 2-3 minutes on medium to low heat. When the centre is cooked and the edges begin to detach from the sides of the pan, remove the appam from the pan. Do not flip. Repeat with the remaining batter.
5. Serve hot with any gravy, vegetable stew or sweetened coconut milk.

Green Dosa

•••

INGREDIENTS
1 cup parboiled* rice, washed
1 cup sprouted green gram (moong dal)*, washed
(See 'Sprouts – the Power Food' section in the 'Techniques' section)
¼ cup split black gram, skinless (dhuli urad dal)*, washed
1 tsp split Bengal gram (dhuli chana dal)*, washed
1 tsp split pigeon peas (dhuli toovar dal)*, washed
½ tsp fenugreek seeds*
1 bunch coriander leaves*, fresh, trimmed, washed, chopped
1" piece ginger, chopped
Black pepper powder to taste
Butter / oil to cook
Salt to taste

METHOD
1. Soak the rice in 3-4 cups of water for 6 hours. Similarly soak the green gram, black gram, Bengal gram, and pigeon peas along with fenugreek seeds in 2 cups of water for 2 hours.
2. Grind the coriander leaves and ginger to a smooth paste, adding a little salt and water as needed.

> • *Use the edge of a spoon instead of a vegetable peeler to effectively remove the ginger skin from the rough corners. Ginger can be crushed either with a mortar and pestle, or on a cutting board with a rolling pin.*
> • *Grinding the dal separately from the rice ensures that it becomes fluffy, and also helps in hastening fermentation.*
> • *If sprouted green gram is not available, 2 cups of rice can be used instead.*

115

3. Drain the water from the rice and dals. Grind the rice and dal separately into smooth pastes.

4. Mix the green paste (coriander and ginger) with the rice and dal pastes, adding sufficient water to make a dosa-like batter. (When a spoon is dipped into the batter, it should thickly coat the spoon.) Add salt to taste.

5. Allow the batter to ferment for 4-5 hours. Stir in pepper powder.

6. Make dosas from this batter, using butter / oil on the griddle (tawa) to make them crispy.

Ragi (Finger Millet) Dosa

INGREDIENTS
1 cup ragi* (finger millet) flour
1 cup black gram flour (coarse dhuli urad dal* flour)
9–10 coriander leaves*, finely chopped
1 tsp cumin* seeds (optional)
8-10 curry leaves, torn in half
Oil to cook
Salt to taste

- *For a sweet ragi dosa, add jaggery*- and cardamom* to the batter before letting it rest for 2 hours. Also add grated cashews and grated coconut instead of the seasonings and curry leaves.*
- *Coarse black gram flour can be replaced with idli* flour. To omit the 2 hours rest time in step 2, add ¼ cup sour curd to the batter. Allow it to rest for 15-20 minutes and then proceed with cooking.*
- *Make your own ragi flour: this can be done by dry-roasting the ragi on a pan and then grinding into a flour in a food processor.*
  A more nutritious flour can be made from sprouted ragi.
  (See 'Sprouts - the Power Food' in the 'Techniques' section.)
  Dry roast, cool and then grind into a flour.

117

METHOD

1. Put both the flours in a deep vessel and add water slowly, mixing continuously, to make a dosa-like batter (When a spoon is dipped into the batter, it should thickly coat the spoon).
2. Allow the batter to rest for 2 hours.
3. Add the coriander leaves, cumin seeds, salt, and hand-torn curry leaves to the batter. Make dosas, using oil as required, on a hot dosa tawa (flat pan). (Use ghee instead of oil for a richer taste.)

Ragi Palak and Vegetable Dosa

INGREDIENTS

1 bunch spinach (palak), fresh, trimmed, cleaned
2 cups ragi* (finger millet) flour
1 cup dosa flour*
1 cabbage, small, finely chopped
4 carrots, peeled, finely chopped
4 tbsp rice flour
Salt to taste

For the Seasoning

1 tsp oil
1 tsp mustard seeds
1 tbsp split Bengal gram (dhuli chana dal)*
1 tbsp split black gram, skinless (dhuli urad dal)*
10-12 curry leaves

METHOD

1. Cook the spinach in a pan with a few drops of oil until soft. Drain the water and chop it.
2. Add the ragi flour, dosa flour, and salt to taste; mix well, adding water slowly, until it reaches the consistency of dosa batter.

• *It is better to allow refrigerated dosa batter to reach normal temperature before making dosas.*

119

(When a spoon is dipped into the batter, it should thickly coat the spoon. Ensure the batter is not too thin, or it will be difficult to add the chopped vegetables later.)

3. Allow the batter to ferment for 2 hours. (In cold places, fermentation takes longer. It is best to cover it with a lid and place it in a warm place, like near an oven or microwave or under a warm lamp.)

4. Heat the oil in a pan; add the mustard seeds. As they begin to splutter, add the dals and curry leaves and sauté for ½ a minute.

5. Add the spinach, cabbage, and carrot and cook until soft. Mix the rice flour into the pan. (Mixing rice flour will ensure the vegetables disperse throughout in the batter, rather than sinking to the bottom of the bowl.)

6. Add the sautéed vegetables to the fermented batter and mix well.

7. Heat a dosa tawa (flat pan); spread a little oil and pour a ladleful of batter in a round shape. Make a few holes in the centre. Pour a little oil on the sides and in the centre and cover with a domed lid. Cook on low heat. (Use ghee instead of oil for a richer taste.)

8. Flip the dosa and cook the other side until it is nice and crispy around the edges.

9. Serve with sambar* or chutney.

Ragi (Finger Millet) Idiyappam (String Hoppers)

· ·

INGREDIENTS
1 cup ragi* (finger millet) flour
1 cup rice flour
1 tsp oil
½ coconut, grated
6–8 broken cashews
2–3 green cardamom* pods
Powdered jaggery* or sugar to taste
Salt to taste

METHOD
1. Put both the flours in a deep bowl and add the oil.
2. Add salt, and using hot water, knead into a soft dough.
3. Cover and allow it to rest for 10 minutes.
4. Slightly oil an *idiyappam** machine (or a *murukku* making machine). Use a mould with small holes, being sure to slightly oil the disc as well as the idli* mould you plan to use.

> • *After step 8, this idiyappam can also be made savoury, by salting and serving with kurma, stew or coconut-based gravies. Cooked vegetables and seasoning can also be added to make an uppuma.*

121

5. Press the dough through the mould. Neatly pile up the long strings in a greased idli mould.
6. Steam the filled trays in the idli maker for 10–12 minutes.
7. Remove and transfer onto a serving plate.
8. Sprinkle the coconut over the string hoppers.
9. Roast the broken cashews and cardamom and add. Sprinkle the powdered jaggery.
10. Mix everything lightly and serve.

Sago Uppuma

••

INGREDIENTS
1¼ cups sago*, large-sized, washed well to remove dust particles, soaked overnight
10-12 French beans, stringed, finely chopped
1 carrot, medium-sized, peeled, grated
1 potato, medium-sized, peeled, chopped into bite-sized pieces
¼ cup groundnuts, roasted, coarsely ground
2"-piece coconut (optional), fresh, grated
1 tbsp lemon juice
Coriander leaves*, fresh, as desired
Salt to taste

For the Seasoning

2 tbsp oil
1 tsp mustard seeds
1 tsp cumin* seeds
10-12 curry leaves
1 tsp turmeric powder*

- *Move the sago pearls around with a fork while soaking, to facilitate even soaking. By morning, the sago should have become swollen, like separate soft pearls. To check if the sago has softened, press it with your fingers. If the centre is still hard, let it soak for longer. The sago should be clear and transparent, without any lumps. Soaking the sago makes it at least twice its original size. If it is not possible to soak the sago overnight, wash the sago and soak it for 2-2½ hours.*
- *This dish is often served with curd, chutney or pickle. If desired, add red chilli powder.*

123

METHOD

1. Drain the sago into a colander and keep it aside. (Some varieties of sago will need to be spread on a dry cloth for all the water to drain.)

2. For the seasoning, heat the oil in a pan and add the mustard seeds. When they begin to splutter, add the cumin seeds, curry leaves, and turmeric powder. (If you wish, you can add dhuli urad dal* or dhuli chana dal* in this step.)

3. Add the beans, carrots, and potato pieces and sprinkle water. Cover the pan with a lid and cook until soft.

4. Add the sago. Sprinkle a little water and salt and stir for about 5 minutes. Stir gently, but firmly, ensuring that the sago does not stick to the pan.

5. Switch off the stove. Add the roasted groundnuts and coconut; mix well.

6. Add the lemon juice and mix well.

7. Serve hot, garnished with coriander leaves.

Maize Sooji Uppuma

INGREDIENTS

3 cups maize *sooji** (cornmeal)
3 tbsp oil
1 tsp mustard seeds
5 red chillies
1 carrot, medium-sized, peeled, finely chopped
7-8 French beans, stringed, finely chopped
1 green capsicum, small, finely chopped
2 tbsp green peas
½ tsp turmeric powder*
¼ cup mint leaves, fresh, shredded
1 tsp lemon juice
2" piece coconut, grated
10-12 broken cashews, roasted
4-5 coriander leaves, fresh
Salt to taste

METHOD

1. Place the maize sooji in a pan and dry roast until it is warm and fragrant. Remove from the pan. Roasting this well ensures that the uppuma is not sticky.
2. Heat the oil in a pan. Add the mustard seeds. As they begin to splutter, add the red chillies.

• *If desired, add some ghee before serving.*

3. Add the carrot, beans, capsicum, peas, turmeric powder, and mint; sauté for 1 minute.
4. Add the maize sooji to the cooking pan, mix thoroughly coating all the vegetables.
5. Add the boiled, salted water to the maize and vegetable mixture, 1 cup or ladleful at a time. Stir the uppuma thoroughly between each addition of water so that no lumps are formed. The water will be absorbed in a couple of minutes, and the mixture will be cooked. It should not stick to the bottom of the pan. Turn off the stove and add the lemon juice. Stir well.
6. Garnish with the coconut, cashews, and coriander leaves. Serve hot.

Bottle Gourd Muthiya (Steamed Dumplings)

••

INGREDIENTS

1 bottle gourd*, large-sized, washed, peeled, cut lengthwise, grated
1½ cups coarse wheat flour (atta)
2 tbsp gram flour*
2 tsp sugar
½ tsp turmeric powder*
4–5 sprigs coriander leaves*, fresh, finely chopped
A generous pinch baking soda
Curd as required
Coconut, grated, as desired
Salt to taste

- *Bottle gourd peel can be used in chutneys, fried and added into stir-fry dishes or made into bhaji.*
- *This dish is often served topped with grated coconut and roasted sesame seeds, along with mint-coriander* or tamarind*-date chutney.*
- *If desired, add red chilli powder or garam masala* in step 2.*

For the seasoning

5 tbsp oil
1 tsp mustard seeds
10–12 curry leaves
1 tbsp white sesame seeds (optional)

METHOD

1. Squeeze the grated bottle gourd and reserve the juices. For better results, salt the grated bottle gourd and keep aside for 15–20 minutes, then squeeze – this reduces the water and also seasons the vegetable.
2. Add the coarse wheat flour, gram flour, sugar, turmeric powder, salt, baking soda, half of the coriander leaves, and 3 tbsp oil. Knead lightly to incorporate the ingredients. Add a little curd and bottle gourd juice (from step 1) and knead into a soft dough. Let the dough sit for about 10 minutes. (The dough should not be too thin. It should be of medium consistency – should not drip from a spoon very easily. If the dough becomes sticky, add more gram flour to make it soft.)
3. Shape the dough into thick, long, cylindrical pieces resembling bananas. Apply a bit of oil on your hands beforehand, to make the shaping easier.
4. Put in a steamer for about 20 minutes. Insert a knife or toothpick to check if they are ready. If ready, the toothpick / knife will come out clean. Remove from heat and allow to cool. Slice into roundels.
5. For the seasoning, heat 2 tbsp oil in a pan and add the mustard seeds. When they splutter, add the curry leaves. Add the steamed roundels and sauté until crispy.
6. Add the sesame seeds (optional) and sauté until golden and crisp.
7. Serve hot, garnished with fresh coriander and grated coconut.

Apple-Tomato Chutney

● ●

INGREDIENTS

500 g apples, peeled, roughly chopped
150 g tomatoes, chopped
45 g raisins
50 g brown sugar
½ cup lemon juice
3 cloves*
½" stick cinnamon*
3 green cardamom* pods
1 tbsp red chilli powder
½ tsp black pepper powder
Salt to taste

METHOD

1. Place the apples in a mixer. Add the tomatoes, raisins, brown sugar, and lemon juice. Grind to a paste. Transfer the paste to a thick-bottomed pan.
2. Place the cloves, cinnamon stick, cardamom, red chilli powder, and pepper powder in a piece of clean white cloth and tie the cloth into a bundle. Place the bundle in the pan, along with the paste and salt to taste.
3. Cook on low heat until the chutney is thick. Remove from heat and allow to cool. Remove the spice bundle.
4. Store the chutney in a clean, glass bottle. It can remain good for 10 days at room temperature. This makes a good side dish for bread, chapatti* and dosas.

Butter Fruit (Avocado) Chutney

INGREDIENTS
1 butter fruit (avocado), halved, seeds discarded, chopped
½ tsp black pepper powder
1 tbsp lemon juice
1 tsp olive oil
Salt to taste

METHOD
1. Place the butter fruit in a mixer.
2. Add the salt, black pepper powder, and lemon juice; grind to a smooth paste.
3. Transfer into a bowl, mix in the olive oil and serve.

- *This dish can also be made into the popular dip guacamole. Add a few tbsp of cabbage, finely diced capsicum, and coriander leaves*. It can be used to dress salads or as a dip for vegetable pieces.*

Ridge Gourd Peel Chutney

. . . .

INGREDIENTS

1 cup ridge gourd* *(peerkangai)* peels
2 tbsp oil
1 tsp split Bengal gram (dhuli chana dal)*
¼ tsp split black gram, skinless (dhuli urad dal)*
3–4 red chillies
½ coconut, fresh, grated
½"-piece ginger, peeled, chopped
1 tamarind*, small ball
Salt to taste

METHOD

1. Heat 1 tbsp oil in a pan. Add the dals and red chillies and sauté for 2 minutes until the dals turn brown and fragrant.
2. Add the coconut to the mix and sauté for a couple of more minutes.
3. Add the ginger and tamarind. Mix everything well and remove from heat. Allow it to cool.
4. Heat the remaining oil in another pan; add the ridge gourd peel and sauté for 1–2 minutes. Allow it to cool.
5. Put the dal mixture, ridge gourd peels, and salt in the jar of a mixer and grind to make a chutney.
6. Serve with rice or chapattis*.

> • *You can also use the whole ridge gourd along with the peel. Cut into pieces and sauté for 1–2 minutes and then grind along with the dal mix.*

131

Toovar Dal Chutney

INGREDIENTS
¼ cup split pigeon peas (dhuli toovar dal)*
2 red chillies
7–8 curry leaves
¼ coconut, fresh, grated
1 tamarind*, small ball
Salt to taste

METHOD
1. Put the pigeon peas in a pan and roast on medium heat until they turn light brown and fragrant.
2. Add the red chillies and curry leaves; roast for 2-3 minutes.
3. Add the grated coconut. Toss for couple of minutes.
4. Add the tamarind and salt to taste; cook on low heat for a minute.
5. Cool and transfer into the jar of a mixer.
6. Add a little water and grind to a chutney.

| • *Excellent with hot boiled rice and ghee.*

Tangy Mango Chutney

••

INGREDIENTS

1 raw mango, small, washed, cut flesh off the mango seed,
chopped into cubes
½ cup coconut, grated
1 sprig (6-8 leaves) curry leaves
½ tsp cumin* seeds
2–4 red chillies
Salt to taste

METHOD

1. Place the mango cubes in the jar of the blender and pulse quickly.
2. Add the remaining ingredients: coconut, curry leaves, cumin seeds, red chillies, and salt; blend to a semi-coarse texture. If absolutely needed, at the very end, a little water may be streamed into the blender while grinding to achieve a chutney-like consistency.

Mango-Curd Chutney

••

INGREDIENTS

1 raw mango, small, washed, cut flesh off the mango seed,
chopped into cubes
2 tbsp + ½ tsp mustard seeds
4 red chillies
1 cup coconut, grated
1 cup curd
1 tsp coconut oil
A few curry leaves
Salt to taste

METHOD

1. Coarsely grind 2 tbsp mustard seeds, red chillies, and salt together in a blender or mixie. Add the coconut and cut mango; blend.
2. Add the curd and blend well to a smooth consistency.
3. Heat a small pan or wok over high heat; add the coconut oil. Once the oil is hot (but not smoking), add the remaining mustard seeds. Once they begin to splutter, add the curry leaves and cook just until blistered.
4. Add the tempering to the chutney, mix well and serve.

Green Tamarind Chutney

. . . .

INGREDIENTS
10–12 green tamarind* pods, fresh, washed, top skin and side
fibres removed
4 red chillies
½ tsp cumin* seeds
1 tbsp jaggery*
½ tsp mustard seeds
Oil for tempering
Salt to taste

METHOD
1. Grind the red chillies, cumin seeds, jaggery, and salt to a coarse
   powder using a blender or mixie.
2. Add the tamarind and blend to a coarse powder.
3. Heat a little oil in a pan. Once very hot, splutter the mustard
   seeds.
4. Add this tempering to the chutney and mix well. Serve.

Groundnut Chutney

• •

INGREDIENTS
¼ cup groundnuts
2 tbsp oil
5–7 red chillies
1 tamarind*, marble-sized piece, soaked in water
1½ tbsp jaggery*
½ cup coconut, grated
¼ cup coriander leaves*
¼ tsp mustard seeds
½ tsp cumin* seeds
Salt to taste

METHOD
1. Heat 1 tbsp oil in a pan; add the red chillies and groundnuts and roast lightly, until the groundnuts turn light brown in colour. Allow it to cool.
2. Grind the groundnuts, chillies, tamarind, jaggery, coconut, coriander leaves, and salt (to taste) to a coarse paste. If needed, add a little oil to adjust the consistency of the chutney.
3. Heat 1 tbsp oil in a pan. Add the mustard seeds. Once they have spluttered, add the cumin seeds and allow it to lightly toast.
4. Add this tempering to the chutney and mix well. Serve.

Drumstick Leaf Chutney

• •

INGREDIENTS

½ cup drumstick leaves*, washed, drained, pat-dried with tea towel
2 tbsp oil
¼ tsp cumin* seeds
5-7 red chillies
¼ tsp split Bengal gram (dhuli chana dal)*
¼ tsp split Black gram (dhuli urad dal)*
¼ tsp mustard seeds
1 tamarind*, marble-sized piece, soaked in water
¼ cup coconut, grated
Salt to taste

METHOD

1. Heat 1 tbsp oil in a pan; roast the cumin seeds, red chillies, and dals. Remove from the pan and set aside in a separate plate.
2. Add the drumstick leaves to the pan with 1 tbsp oil, and sauté until soft. Allow it to cool.
3. Remove the whole chillies from the plate, and grind along with the wilted drumstick leaves, tamarind, coconut, and salt to a slightly coarse paste. Add the dals from the plate and grind for a few seconds, maintaining the slightly coarse texture.

Snacks
and Sweets

If you're looking for a yummy snack or trying to satisfy your sweet tooth, you've come to the right place. While at first glance, some of the items may seem complicated to make, the recipes are simple and easy to follow. Try and see!

Banana Roti

•••

INGREDIENTS
2–3 ripe bananas, peeled, chopped
1 cup milk
2 tbsp powdered sugar
3 cups wheat flour (atta)
2 tbsp oil
½ tsp salt

METHOD
1. Blend the bananas in a blender.
2. Add the milk and sugar and whisk until smooth. Set aside.
3. In a large bowl, combine the wheat flour and salt. Add the oil and then the banana mixture.
4. Mix everything into pliable dough and let it rest for about half an hour.
5. Divide the dough into small portions and roll into balls.
6. Roll out into small chapattis* or *rotis*.
7. Roast them on a griddle (tawa) until golden flecks show on both sides.
8. Serve warm.

- *This can be served drizzled with honey, sweet condensed milk, ghee*, powdered sugar, powdered jaggery* or even chocolate syrup. A little grated coconut can either top the roti or be stuffed into the dough before step 4.*
- *Another variation common in Thai cuisine (also known as Thai Banana Pancake) is to roll the dough, then add chopped bananas in the centre and wrap the dough around it. This can be cooked or fried on the griddle. This makes for an ideal breakfast item.*

Date Balls

• •

INGREDIENTS
20 black dates, deseeded
10 cashews, coarsely crushed or chopped
6 almonds, coarsely crushed or chopped
1 tbsp pumpkin seeds*
½ dry coconut, grated

METHOD
1. Put the dates in an open vessel and mash with your hands.
2. Add the cashews and almonds along with the pumpkin seeds. Mix everything well using your hands.
3. Divide the mixture into bite-sized portions and shape into balls. (If you wish, you can make these into bars and wrap it for later, like a granola bar.)
4. Put the coconut on a plate.
5. Roll the date balls on the coconut ensuring that each one is well coated.
6. Serve.

• *If the dates are too dry or difficult to mash, you can soak the dates in hot water for a few minutes to soften them. This water sweetened by the dates can be added to juices or smoothies.*
• *Almonds, walnuts, cashews, pistachios, sunflower seeds, cacao nibs or oats can be added in step 2. You can even add spices and flavours like cardamom* powder, cinnamon*, vanilla or cocoa.*
• *For a different touch, before serving, you can brush the balls with grated coconut or cocoa powder or top it with a cashew nut. With refrigeration, this has a shelf life of 10 days.*

American-style Snack Mix

●●●

INGREDIENTS
1 cup puffed rice
1 cup puffed jowar*
2 cups cornflakes
1 cup Asian-style rice crackers
¾ cup groundnuts, roasted
½ cup cashews, roasted
4 tbsp ghee*
¼ tsp nigella seeds*
¼ tsp mango powder *(amchur)*
Masala of your choice *(See tip)*
1½–2 tbsp doy sauce

METHOD
1. Preheat the oven to 120°C / 250°F.
2. In a large bowl, combine all the puffed items, cornflakes, crackers, groundnuts, and cashews. Any combination of items can be used, as long as the total amount of cereal crackers equals 5 cups; 6¼ including the nuts.
3. In a small saucepan, bring the ghee up to medium-high heat.

• *We recommend masala with coriander, chilli, fennel, cinnamon, pepper, turmeric, clove, cardamom, cumin, and fenugreek. See the index to know more about these spices.*

4. Add the nigella seeds and let them splutter.
5. Remove the pan from the heat and stir in the mango powder, masala, and soy sauce.
6. Pour the hot ghee mixture over the dry ingredients and toss until everything is fully coated.
7. Transfer the contents of the bowl onto a large baking sheet, spreading out the snack as much as possible. Roast for approximately 1 hour (or until everything has become golden and toasty), stirring every 15 minutes.
8. Allow to cool and store in an airtight container.

Granola

· ·

INGREDIENTS
2 coconuts, fresh, grated
¼ cup dates, finely chopped
2 cups oats
1 cup nuts (cashews, walnuts or almonds)
1 tsp cinnamon* powder
½ cup sunflower oil
2 tbsp maple syrup (or jaggery syrup)

METHOD
1. Put the coconut and dates in a large, deep bowl with the oats and nuts.
2. In a separate bowl, mix the cinnamon powder, oil, and maple syrup well together.

- *Instead of sunflower oil, use melted butter for a richer taste (step 2).*
- *Granola can be had dry, as a snack, or served with sliced bananas and milk or curd as breakfast. It also makes a wonderful topping for ice cream.*
- *Granola can be varied and altered as per individual preference. Many add chocolate (after cooling) or cacao nibs.*
- *Other additions include:*
  Nuts: walnuts, cashews, almonds or chopped groundnuts
  Seeds: sunflower, pumpkin, flax, ash gourd or sesame
  Dry fruit: raisins, sultanas, figs, apricots, apple or cherries
  Spices and flavours (into the mixture described in step 3): vanilla or almond extract, nutmeg, clove, ginger powder, allspice, peanut butter
  Sweeteners: brown rice syrup, jaggery syrup

3. Pour this over the oats mixture and stir well until the oats are evenly coated.
4. Preheat oven to 100°C / 212°F. Grease 2 rectangular baking trays with a little oil.
5. Pour the oat mixture onto the baking trays.
6. Bake in the oven for about 1½ hours, or until toasted, stirring gently every 15–20 minutes to prevent sticking.
7. Remove, cool, and store in an airtight container.

Banana Pancakes

. . . .

INGREDIENTS
¾ cup refined flour (*maida*)*
¼ cup wheat flour (atta) or Sanjeevini* powder
1 tsp baking powder
¼ tsp salt
1 tbsp flaxseed* powder
3 tbsp water
1 tbsp or more oil or ghee*
1½ tbsp jaggery* syrup (thick; 2 tbsp if syrup is thinner)
½ tsp vanilla extract
2 bananas, peeled, sliced into ½"-rounds
Cinnamon* to sprinkle (optional)

METHOD
1. Sift together the refined flour, wheat flour or Sanjeevini, baking powder, and salt into a medium-sized bowl.
2. In a larger bowl, whisk together the flaxseed powder and water until it emulsifies. (This can also be done in a mixie.) Continue to whisk in the remaining wet ingredients: oil / ghee, jaggery syrup, and vanilla extract.
3. Add the dry ingredients to the wet ingredients, a heaped spoonful at a time, stirring constantly. Mix in the vanilla extract. The batter should be the consistency of idli* batter. Add a little extra water, if needed.

- *Excellent if served with freshly sliced bananas, thick warm jaggery syrup and a few praline cashews. Pancakes are typically a breakfast or brunch item, but also make for a special mid-day treat.*

4. Heat a heavy-bottomed skillet or griddle (tawa) over medium heat. Once it comes to temperature, pour a little ghee onto the hot surface and swirl it around.

5. Place a quarter cup of batter, at a time, on the griddle, and allow it to cook for 2–3 minutes. (You can make as many pancakes at a time as your cooking surface will allow – just make sure the spoonfuls of cake batter don't touch.)

6. The cakes are ready to flip once the batter surface begins to lose its sheen and bubbles appear to form at the outside edges of the batter rounds. If desired, place a few banana slices on each pancake, sprinkle with cinnamon, and flip.

7. Continue to cook until the bottom is also golden brown. Remove from heat.

8. Serve warm.

Praline Cashews (Vanilla Chikki)

INGREDIENTS
2½ cups cashews (whole or pieces)
4 tbsp (+ preparation) ghee*
1¼ cups jaggery* or brown sugar
1 tsp vanilla extract
Salt to taste

METHOD
1. Grease a metal plate or tray with a very thin coating of ghee and set aside.
2. In a heavy-bottomed skillet, roast the cashews over medium heat, until golden and fragrant. Remove from pan and set aside.
3. In the same skillet, add the 4 tbsp ghee and continue to melt over medium heat. Add the jaggery or brown sugar. Stir frequently.
4. Allow the jaggery to bubble and caramelize. Once it deepens in colour, stir in the vanilla and salt. Remove from heat. (The sugar can burn easily, so keep a close eye on the pan.) Add the nuts and mix well.
5. Pour the hot nut mixture on the greased plate (spreading out the nuts as much as possible) and allow it to cool.
6. Once cooled, crack apart into bite-sized pieces and serve.

• *This can be eaten as a snack or crumbled as a garnish for dessert dishes. Extras may be stored in an airtight container.*

Spiced Orange Compote

· ·

INGREDIENTS

4 Nagpur oranges (or any sweet juicy variety of oranges), peeled, segments separated and seeds removed
¾ cup jaggery* syrup
6 cloves*
1"-piece ginger, peeled
1 bay leaf
1 whole star anise*
1 tsp lemon juice
⅓ cup sultanas

METHOD

1. In a medium saucepan, warm the jaggery syrup. *(See 'Jaggery – The Medicinal Sugar' in the 'Techniques' section.)*
2. Add the cloves, ginger, bay leaf, and star anise. Allow the spices to boil gently until the syrup is reduced to ½ cup. Add the lemon juice and remove from heat.
3. Place all the separated orange segments and the sultanas in a bowl. Pour the warm syrup over the fruit, using a strainer to collect the whole spices and prevent them from falling into the dish.
4. Allow the mixture to chill in the refrigerator for at least one hour and serve.

• *This can be served over curd or ice cream as a dessert topping, or as a fruity accompaniment to cake or biscuits.*

Banana Halwa

. . . .

INGREDIENTS
5 Kerala bananas
300 g jaggery*
1 tsp green cardamom* powder
3 tbsp ghee*

METHOD
1. Cook the bananas in a pressure cooker. Remove and cool. Peel and make a paste using a blender. Keep aside until needed.
2. Pour 1 cup of water in a pan and add the jaggery. Heat until it dissolves completely and then filter it to remove the impurities. Place the filtered jaggery on heat and cook until a syrup of one-string consistency is formed. (One-string consistency can be checked by lifting a ladle from the syrup. If the syrup drops in a single string – not two or three – it has reached the proper consistency.)
3. Add the mashed bananas to the syrup and cook, stirring continuously, until the halwa begins to leave the sides of the pan.
4. Add the cardamom powder and ghee; mix well.
5. Remove from heat.
6. Cool and serve.

Sooji Halwa

• •

INGREDIENTS
¼ cup white sooji*
1¼ cups water
½ cup sugar
5 pinches cardamom* powder
3 tbsp ghee*
5 cashews
10 raisins

METHOD
1. Roast the sooji with 1 tbsp ghee in a pan until the colour turns slightly dark and gives a roasted aroma. Set aside.
2. Boil the water and sugar together till the sugar is totally dissolved. Add the cardamom powder to the syrup.
3. Slowly add this sugar syrup to the roasted sooji while stirring continuously. Add 1½ tbsp ghee to the pan and keep stirring until it starts to thicken. Ensure no lumps are formed.
4. Cook the halwa on low heat until it leaves the sides of the pan.
5. Meanwhile, heat the remaining ghee in a small pan and fry the cashews and raisins.
6. Add the cashews and raisins to the halwa along with the ghee and serve.

Ash Gourd Halwa

••

INGREDIENTS

300–400 g ash gourd* (white pumpkin), peeled, grated
1 cup ghee*
10 cashews
1 cup sugar
1 tsp green cardamom* powder

METHOD

1. Squeeze the grated ash gourd pulp by hand to remove excess liquid or, alternatively, allow the pulp to sit in a sieve / colander for some time until the juice runs out.
2. Heat the ghee in a pan; sauté the cashews until golden brown. Remove the cashews with a slotted spoon and keep aside until needed.
3. To the same ghee, add the grated ash gourd and sauté for 3–4 minutes. Add the sugar and cardamom powder.
4. Cook, stirring continuously, until the halwa begins to leave the sides of the pan and becomes a homogenous mass. Add the fried cashews and mix well.
5. Cool and serve.

Coconut Mango Crisp

....

INGREDIENTS

5 cups ripe mangoes, washed, peeled, diced, save the juice
1 tbsp corn flour (corn starch)
1 tbsp lemon juice
1" piece ginger, grated, save the juice
¼ cup + ½ cup jaggery* shaved
1 cup rolled oats
½ cup almonds, slivered
¾ cup dried coconut, shredded or powdered
3 tbsp Sanjeevini* powder
3 tbsp wheat flour (atta)
¼ cup ghee* / coconut oil, cooled
A pinch of salt

- *This dish is traditionally baked in an oven. If your kitchen does not have an oven, you can either briefly cook the fruit filling on the stovetop for 20 minutes after completing step 5, or, alternatively, leave the mangoes raw. Omit the corn starch if the mangoes will not be cooked. To complete the dish, toast the topping mixture (step 5), in a sauté pan over medium-high heat until the almonds and coconut become brown and fragrant. Layer the fruit and granola-like crunch in small serving glasses and garnish as described.*
- *Atta can be substituted for the Sanjeevini powder - a total of 6 tbsp flour is needed for the recipe.*

METHOD

1. Preheat the oven to 180°C / 350°F. Lightly grease an 8" × 8" baking pan or dish with ghee or coconut oil. Set aside.
2. In a mixing bowl, whisk together the corn flour, lemon juice, ginger (+ juice), and ¼ cup jaggery. Continue to stir until the corn flour and jaggery are dissolved.
3. Toss the mangoes into the mixing bowl and thoroughly coat the fruit.
4. In a separate bowl, combine the rolled oats, almonds, shredded or powdered coconut, Sanjeevini powder, wheat flour, and salt. Mix.
5. Add the ghee / coconut oil. Gently mix all the ingredients together, until the topping begins to form pea-size clusters. (The clusters will form more readily if the oil or ghee is cold and you 'cut' – or break the larger piece of it into smaller chunks by mashing it into the dry ingredients with a fork; if the fat is warmer, the topping will still taste delicious, but will have a 'sand-like' rather than 'gravel-like' appearance.)
6. Pour the fruit mixture into the greased pan. Sprinkle on the topping mixture created in step 5. Place in the heated oven and bake for 40 minutes.
7. Remove and allow to cool. Serve as a dessert on its own, or top with the vanilla version of *elaichi* crème.

Date Roll

....

INGREDIENTS

15 dates
15 whole cashews
250 g refined flour (maida)*
¼ tsp baking powder
125 g powdered sugar
125 g butter
4–5 drops vanilla essence

METHOD

1. Preheat the oven to 180°C / 350°F.
2. Remove the seeds from the dates and stuff one cashew nut inside each date. The larger end of the cashew should be visible outside the date.
3. Sift the flour with the baking powder. Keep aside.
4. Put powdered sugar and butter in a bowl and beat until light and creamy. Add the vanilla essence and mix.
5. Add the flour, little by little, and mix well until a dough is formed.
6. Divide the dough into 15 portions and shape each into a ball.
7. Using the thumb, make a dent in the middle of the ball.
8. Place a stuffed date inside the ball, ensuring that it is only half covered with the dough and the cashew is still visible.
9. Place on a greased baking tray at some distance from each other.
10. Bake for 25 minutes in the oven and remove.
11. Cool and serve.

Elaichi Crème

•••

INGREDIENTS
2¼ cups raw cashews, rinsed, soaked for 4–6 hours or overnight
2 lemons
½ cup jaggery* syrup, thick
2/3 cup coconut oil
¼ cup water
¼ tsp cardamom* seeds, crushed
½ tsp vanilla extract (optional)
A pinch of salt

METHOD
1. Drain the cashews and place in a mixie, grind to a paste-like consistency, adding ¼ cup water little by little. (This should look a bit like peanut butter, only much smoother.)
2. Add in the juice of the lemons along with the remaining ingredients and continue to blend. (The amount of cardamom, vanilla, and salt can be adjusted as per your individual taste; the salt will help to heighten and contrast the natural sweetness of the other ingredients. Omit the cardamom and increase the vanilla to mimic the flavour of whipped cream.)
3. Garnish with your choice of nuts or raisins and serve.

- *Soaking the cashews until fully hydrated will produce a smoother custard.*
- *The crème can be offered as it is in small dessert dishes or ramekins, or used as a dessert topping for other dishes, or even frozen. When frozen and then thawed, the custard sets and becomes firmer, like the consistency of cheesecake.*

Butter Fruit (Avocado) Pista Pudding

· ·

INGREDIENTS

2 ripe butter fruits, chopped in half lengthwise
5 tbsp pistachios, shelled, roughly chopped
2 tbsp honey
1 tbsp sweet lime juice
½ tsp rose water

METHOD

1. Pop the seed out of the butter fruit. Score the butter fruit flesh in a grid pattern. Scoop the flesh from the shell using a spoon.
2. Place the butter fruit in a mixie; blend until the flesh begins to cream.
3. Add the honey, sweet lime, and rose water; blend until smooth and creamy. Adjust the flavours as desired. (Honey provides a nice, floral sweetness to the dish. The sweet lime offers a citrus note, but most importantly, prevents the butterfruit from darkening and turning brown; lemon and or orange juices can be substituted for the sweet lime.)
4. Transfer the pudding into a separate bowl for mixing. Using a spatula or paddle spoon, fold in 3 tbsp chopped pistachios.
5. Spoon the mixture into serving cups. Garnish with the remaining 2 tbsp chopped pistachios, and your choice of whole mint leaves, a slice of orange with zest or edible rose petals.

Water: Poison or Elixir of Life?

Sadhguru

What you call as 'myself,' what you call as the human structure is essentially the work of a certain 'software'. We know today that software means memory. Whether it is the individual human body or the larger cosmic body, essentially they are made of five elements – earth, water, fire, air and space. All the five elements have a memory of their own. That is the reason they behave the way they are behaving.

Today, particularly in the last few years, much experimentation has been done and it has been found that water has memory – it remembers everything that it touches. We have always known this in our culture and we have been using it in so many ways. Our grandmothers told us we should not drink water or eat food from just anyone's hands; we must always receive it from people who love and care for us. In temples they give you one drop of water, which even a multi-billionaire fights for because you cannot buy that water anywhere. It is water which remembers the Divine. This is what *theerth* is. People want to drink the water so that it reminds them of the divinity within them. The same H_2O can be poison or it can be the elixir of life, depending upon what kind of memory it carries.

Because water has memory, we are very concerned with how we store it. If you keep water in a copper vessel, preferably overnight or at least for four hours, the water acquires a certain quality from the copper which is very good for your liver in particular and your health and energy in general. If water is violently pumped and travels to your house through many turns in lead or plastic pipes, much negativity happens to the water. But while water has memory, it also has a way of unfolding itself back into its original state. If you just leave tap water undisturbed for an hour, the negativity will undo itself.

If you're constantly travelling, if your food is not necessarily controlled, minor poisons are always getting into you in various forms. Copper handles those things for you.

HOW MUCH WATER TO DRINK

Drinking water throughout the day is definitely a bad habit. Doing anything in excess is a problem. This is catching on across the world, but especially in the West you see everyone carrying a water bottle everywhere. Every few minutes they are sipping from it because someone told them, 'Water is good.' By constantly sipping water, you dilute your digestive juices. You will not know when you are hungry and when you are not hungry. And immediately after eating if you drink water, you again dilute the digestive juices and disturb the whole digestive process. Just drink for your thirst requirements and a little bit more – that is all. Don't simply unnecessarily drink water.

Drinking tepid water on an empty stomach early in the morning is a great cleanser. For people who suffer from constipation, tepid water can do a lot. In Yoga, we always say drink tepid water, then do asanas, because it cleanses the system. Drinking about three-fourths to a litre of tepid water early in the morning is beneficial.

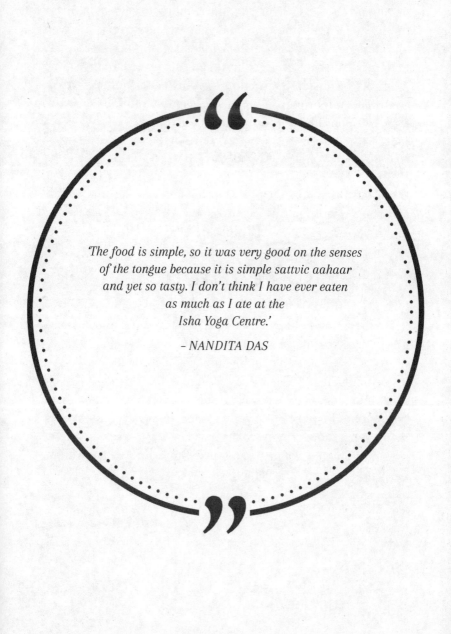

'The food is simple, so it was very good on the senses of the tongue because it is simple sattvic aahaar and yet so tasty. I don't think I have ever eaten as much as I ate at the Isha Yoga Centre.'

– NANDITA DAS

Techniques

The Simplicity of Salad

Making changes to one's diet, no matter how beneficial in the long term, may seem daunting at first. Many of us have been raised eating certain foods cooked in traditional ways. Though we may be willing to try new ingredients, we may not know how to prepare tasty salads with vegetables we've only ever had stewed in curries or blended in chutneys.

The good news is that shifting to a diet containing more natural foods requires much less 'cooking', while the enzymes, vitamins and fibre-rich goodness of the ingredients are preserved. Simply chop and dress! By following a few simple guidelines, ordinary fresh grocery and pantry items can be transformed into the most spectacular of salads.

Salad Dressings

CHOOSING THE RIGHT 'DRESS'

A wide variety of vegetables can be incorporated into a salad, but the choice of dressing is what sets apart one raw dish from another. In its most basic state, salad dressing is a blend of oil and an acidic (sour) element, with salty, sweet, pungent or aromatic elements to balance. When making a dressing, begin with your acids and emulsifying agents (things that will thicken the dressing, including honey). Incorporate the spices and fresh herbs next. Finish by whisking in the oil, incorporating a small, steady amount at a time, stopping once the right creamy consistency is reached. Following are a few classic dressings that will do justice to any salad. Once you become confident in your combining skills, try picking and choosing elements from the table on the next page to create your own customized dressings.

Oils	Olive, coconut (for sweet and fruit salads), almond, sesame, rapeseed / canola
Acids	Lemon juice, lime juice, orange (Nagpur) juice (for sweet and fruit salads); if you don't have fresh juice, amchur* and water, tamarind juice, pomegranate molasses
Salts	Table or sea salt, soy sauce, olive brine
Spices	Black pepper, dried herbs and spices
Emulsifiers	Prepared mustard, vegan mayonnaise, tahini / sesame paste, cashew butter, peanut butter, honey
Fresh herbs	Coriander, parsley, dill, fennel / anise fronds, thyme, basil (tulsi, Thai, purple, or Italian) and lemon / lime / orange zest

NOTES:

About vinegar: Though vinegar is certainly sour and often less expensive than fresh fruit juice, it is not considered to be positive pranic. For that reason, at the ashram and during Isha programmes, we choose to use citrus as opposed to other ingredients which might be less supportive or may aggravate the system.

Consistency of the dressing: Any dressing made by pouring oil into a blender or mixer will create a creamy, mayonnaise-like consistency as additional air is whipped into the mixture. If you prefer a thinner, vinaigrette-like dressing, grind the fruits in the blender, but incorporate all the other ingredients (especially the oil) by hand, using a whisk or wide spoon.

Classic Lemon Juice and Olive Oil Dressing

INGREDIENTS
2 lemons
½ cup olive oil
Black pepper, coarsely ground, to taste
Salt to taste

METHOD
1. In a small bowl, whisk together juice of the lemons, salt and pepper.
2. Holding the measuring cup of olive oil above the bowl, pour the oil in a thin, steady stream, whisking constantly.
3. Continue whisking until the mixture appears slightly creamy and no whole droplets of oil can be seen.

Uses: Particularly good for green leaf salads, and those using tomatoes, cucumber, capsicum, zucchini, squash / gourds.

Change it Up: This is a classic, all-purpose Lebanese-style dressing. For an Italian twist, finely minced red capsicum, parsley, green olive, and a half-spoonful of honey can also be added at step 1. To make it more Greek, add oregano (and even a little feta cheese) to step 1.

Sweet Salad Dressing

INGREDIENTS
1 orange
1 lemon or lime
2 tbsp honey
½ cup olive oil
Black pepper, coarsely ground, to taste
Salt to taste

METHOD

1. In a small bowl, whisk together the juice of the orange and lemon along with the honey, salt, and pepper.
2. Holding the measuring cup of olive oil above the bowl, pour the oil in a thin, steady stream, whisking constantly. (Refer to step 3 from the previous recipe, *Classic Lemon Juice and Olive Oil Dressing.*)

Uses: Nicely complements slightly sweet vegetables like carrots, beets, and steamed pumpkin or even fruit salads. It might seem counter-intuitive to add sourness or salt to fruits, but doing this will actually bring out the natural sweetness of the produce. Spinach is also well-suited for sweet dressings.

Variations: Dried fruits such as raisins, sultanas and dates can be soaked in orange juice ahead of time and then minced and added to the salad or blended into the dressing at step 1. Fresh grated coconut can also be added at step 1. Coconut or almond oil may be substituted for olive oil, and white grape, chikoo* (sapota), apple or sweet lime juice can replace the orange juice, as long as there is still a slightly sour quality to the juice (you can also keep some amount of lemon / lime in the recipe).

Asian 'Vinaigrette' Dressing

INGREDIENTS
½ cup gingelly oil*
2–3 tbsp sesame (*til*) seeds
1 orange
1 lemon or lime
2 tbsp honey
1"-piece ginger, fresh, grated / minced
¼ cup soy sauce
Black pepper, coarsely ground, to taste
Salt to taste

METHOD

1. In a small sauté pan, warm the gingelly oil over medium-high heat.
2. Once the oil is hot, add the sesame seeds and cook, stirring continuously, until they begin to splutter and turn honey-coloured. Set aside.
3. In a small bowl, whisk together the juices of the orange and lemon along with the honey, ginger, and black pepper.
4. Whisk in soy sauce. (If soy sauce is exceptionally salty or if it is thick and slightly syrupy, less is needed. If more salt flavour is needed according to your taste, use additional table or sea salt rather than more soy sauce to avoid a briny flavour.)
5. Holding the tempered gingelly oil above the bowl, pour the oil in a thin, steady stream, whisking constantly and incorporating all the toasted seeds. (Refer to step 3 from the earlier recipe *Classic Lemon Juice and Olive Oil Dressing*.)

Uses: An excellent dressing for 'slaw'-style shredded salads. Try a mixture of shredded carrots, cabbage, cucumber, and whole leaf coriander. Add shredded green papaya or raw mango for an extra pucker.

Variations: Add toasted crushed groundnuts, a tbsp of pomegranate molasses, and shredded basil to step 4 for a Thai flavour or omit the molasses and add fresh mint leaves for a Vietnamese flair. If you want a thicker, creamier dressing, start with a ¼ cup of peanut butter in the bowl at the beginning of step 3. Whisk in the juices first along with a pinch of salt until the mixture becomes light and fluffy. Stir in the ginger, honey, and pepper and proceed with the rest of the recipe.

Raw Mango Dressing

INGREDIENTS

2 raw mangoes, peeled, flesh removed, chopped into cubes
$^1/_8$–¼ cup honey

1¼ cups olive oil
1½ tbsp rose water
Black pepper powder to taste
Salt to taste

METHOD
1. Place the mangoes in a blender / mixer. Grind the mangoes to a thick pulp. Add the honey and continue to grind. (The honey is used to balance the sourness of the mango. You may find you require less or more honey, depending on your taste preference.)
2. Pour in the rose water, and sprinkle in salt and pepper.
3. While the blender is still running, stream in the olive oil.
4. Remove from the blender and serve.

Papaya Dressing

INGREDIENTS
½ papaya*, chopped into small chunks (about 1½ cups)
1 guava, chopped into small chunks
2 tbsp honey
½ lime
½ cup olive oil
Black pepper, ground, to taste
Salt to taste

METHOD
1. Place the papaya and guava in a blender / mixer and blend into a smoothie consistency.
2. Add the honey, lime juice, salt, and pepper; continue to blend.
3. With the blades still running, stream in the olive oil.
4. At this point, check the taste – more lime, honey, salt or pepper may be added as per your preference.
5. Toss with salad vegetables and serve.

Jackfruit Dressing

INGREDIENTS

1 cup jackfruit*, diced, seeds removed (about 4-5 kernels)
½ cup cottage cheese (paneer)*
½ cup olive oil
2 chikoos* (sapota), washed, peeled, seeds removed, chopped
¼ cup grapes, washed, halved, seeds removed
½ raw mango, washed, peeled, seed removed, chopped into pieces
1 butter fruit (avocado), washed, cut into half lengthwise, seed removed
1 pomegranate, washed, seeded

METHOD

1. Score the butter fruit flesh using a butter knife, and with a spoon scrape out the yellow-green fruit from the skin.
2. In a blender, combine the cottage cheese, butter fruit and olive oil. Blend until very creamy. Add the jackfruit, chikoos, grapes, mango, and pomegranate. Blend to a thick consistency. Use as required.

Preparation Methods

THE CUT MATTERS

In most of the recipes in this cookbook you will see we have asked you to 'cut (or chop or dice) into small pieces'. While uniformity in ingredient size is needed for even cooking, when it comes to salads, this rule need not apply. A variety of textures and ingredient sizes actually makes raw food more interesting to eat. Experiment with different cuts and chopping methods: for example, try hand-tearing lettuces and fresh, whole herbs (coriander leaves, mint leaves, basil). Though you may choose to cube a cucumber, try shredding carrots and radishes in the same salad. Green beans and celery can be cut on the bias (angled cut), which is not only pretty to look at, but also offers a greater surface area to crunch! Julienned vegetables lend an East Asian flair.

EVEN VEGETABLES LIKE THE SPA TREATMENT SOMETIMES!

When transitioning to a raw diet, you may find that your system has some difficulty digesting certain dense or fibrous produce. Alternatively, you may discover that adding hearty vegetables to salads keeps you satiated for longer. In either case, you may want to consider adding a few lightly cooked ingredients to your raw dishes. To do this, simply follow the blanching method for high-fibre elements such as broccoli, cauliflower, green / French / pole beans or sweet corn:

1. Cut the vegetables into bite-sized pieces. Set aside.
2. Fill a separate bowl with ice-cold water. This will be needed to stop the cooking process later on in step 6.
3. Bring a medium saucepot of lightly salted water to boil.
4. Once the water is rapidly boiling, add the vegetables by the handful. Cook until the colour of the vegetable intensify (e.g. bright green, translucent white or bright yellow), but not beyond. Remove from heat immediately.
5. Using a colander, hand strainer or sieve, remove the cooked vegetables from the pot, shaking off any excess water.
6. Immediately plunge the hot vegetables into the reserved ice-cold water to stop the cooking process. This is known as 'shocking' the vegetables. The now-cooled elements can remain in the cold water until they are ready to be incorporated into the finished salad. Simply drain and use.

TEXTURE, TEXTURE, TEXTURE!

In addition to utilizing cooked elements and non-traditional cutting techniques, you may also find that the most ordinary of salads can be totally transformed by the element of crunch. Nuts, such as cashews, almonds, groundnuts and walnuts, will work perfectly (even in small quantities) and lightly roasting them will add an even greater depth of flavour. Toasted sunflower, pumpkin and squash seeds likewise provide unexpected texture, while sprouts have a snap and a spice all of their own. *(See 'Sprouts – The Power Food'.)*

Seasoning

Seasoning. Tempering. Spluttering. *Tarka. Chaunk. Phoron.* All mean the same.

Every cooking region in India has its own name for this traditional method of roasting spices in ghee* or oil over high heat. Though the terms change with the geography, the technique is found in virtually every local cuisine, serving either as the first layer of flavour for sauces, gravies and masalas, or as the final flourish, drizzled over dishes just before serving. In either case, tempering serves the dual purpose of imparting a nutty richness to the spices, mellowing the pungency of such ingredients as ginger and turmeric and, perhaps most importantly, infusing the cooking oil with a greater depth of flavour than dry spices alone. Spluttering is an easy technique to learn, and once mastered, can be applied not only to dals and curries, but to such things as salad dressings and even to Italian marinara sauce and Asian marinades.

Regardless of their application, all methods of tempering are similar: whole spices and flavour agents are added in quick succession (depending on each ingredient's cooking requirements, i.e., the time it needs) to a few tablespoons of hot oil. Finishing seasonings usually have only a few ingredients (mustard / cumin* seeds, dhuli urad* / chana dal,* curry leaf) and are poured over the dish while the oil and seeds are still sizzling in the pan. Seasonings that appear at the beginning of a recipe help to determine the basic flavour of the dish, and therefore often require a variety of ingredients and steps before the main vegetables and cooking liquids are added to the pot. Either way, traditional seasonings are typically layered in the following sequence:

Hard or foundational flavour seeds / spices	Mustard seeds, whole cumin,* fenugreek,* fennel,* whole coriander,* clove,* *panch phoron,* etc.
Dals	Urad dal,* chana dal* without skins
Aromatics	Curry leaves, whole red chilli, bay leaves
Sauce-base vegetables	Tomatoes, cabbage or celery (as a substitute for onion), ginger
Pungent seasonings or dried spices requiring special attention	Turmeric,* garam masala,* specialty masalas / powders

Extremely hot (but not smoking) oil / ghee is the key to a successful seasoning. Because it is a very quick process needing close attention (the spices can burn almost instantly if not closely monitored and stirred), it is important to set all of your seasoning ingredients out beforehand. Every recipe has its own proportion of spices; as you become comfortable with the process, you are likely to develop your own signature of seasoning flavour. These are the steps:

1. Arrange all the spices needed for the tempering and keep separately either in small, pre-measured dishes or in a masala box. (Have all these ingredients ready at hand: once the spices begin to fry, there will be very little time to look for additional ingredients and the risk of burning the whole batch is very high.)

2. Place a heavy-bottomed skillet or wok (kadhai) over a high gas flame. (While gas heat is preferred – as it gets very hot, quickly – electric and induction burners will work fine. Just ensure that your pan and oil are very hot.)

3. Once hot, add a high-temperature (high smoke-point) oil such as ghee, safflower, coconut, rapeseed or vegetable oil.

4. When the oil is very hot (but not yet smoking), add the first spice – usually mustard seeds.

5. When the mustard seeds sizzle (with little bubbles coming off the now steel-coloured seeds), add your second spice – usually cumin seeds.

6. Once the cumin seeds likewise appear to 'fizz', add any additional spices you may have one by one. These spices could include fenugreek, carom *(ajwain)*, fennel, clove, panch phoron or coriander. (Just remember that the denser the seed / spice is, the longer cooking time it will require, so add denser seeds first and lighter, more papery spices like coriander last.)

7. After all the whole spices are in, add any dals required for the tempering. Cook until just brown on the edges. (Toasting the entire urad dal or chana dal to a golden / dark brown will make the dal extremely hard and unpleasantly crunchy to eat. You may need to lower the heat / flame at this step to prevent overcooking.)

8. Add fresh or dried curry leaves or other aromatics. Sauté until just blistered. (If using as a finishing element, the

seasoning is now done. Transfer the hot oil and spices to the final dish and serve.)

9. If, however, you are making a sauce, add the base vegetables at this point – tomatoes / cabbage / ginger. Cook at a reduced heat (medium) until the vegetables begin to soften and 'melt' together – a pinch or two of salt will encourage this breakdown process.

10. Add any strong-flavoured powders needed at this step (turmeric, coriander-cumin, garam masala) and allow them to cook. Continue as directed by your recipe.

Though usually found in Indian dishes, try using the tempering method any time you wish to get the most flavour out of your cooking oils.

Protein — Power Groundnuts

Groundnuts (or peanuts) are extremely high in protein, anti-oxidants, niacin and minerals. Just a few spoonfuls of nuts a day can provide a vegetarian with a majority of his or her protein needs. Soaking, more so than any other preparation (roasting, cooking), maximizes the groundnut's phytonutrients, bioavailability, and improves its digestibility in the human system. To soak groundnuts, simply:

1. Shell a sufficient amount of raw groundnuts, or purchase already shelled (unroasted) groundnuts. Skins may remain intact. (Approximately 2 tbsp or $1/8$ cup per person per meal, or as required for a specific recipe.)

2. Thoroughly wash the groundnuts (2-3 times), removing any impurities that may arise.
3. Place the groundnuts in a stainless steel or glass bowl.
4. Cover with warm / tepid purified water. The water level should be more than double the depth of the nuts in the bowl. (Adding a little salt to the warm soaking water has been found to reduce the amount of enzyme inhibitors contained in most dried nuts, making them more digestible and their vitamins more readily accessible.)
5. Place a plate or lid over the bowl.
6. Soak for 6-8 hours. Nuts should become visibly plump.
7. Drain off the soaking liquid.
8. Rinse the soaked nuts thoroughly with fresh water and serve.

Groundnuts can be susceptible to aflatoxin, a particular type of toxin produced by fungi. To reduce the potential of this contaminant, refrigerate any unused nuts immediately after a meal, and be sure to rinse soaked nuts thoroughly before re-serving. If the colour or texture of the soaked groundnut has changed, discard it. Leftover nuts can also be boiled and seasoned and can be used to make fantastic sundal, chaat fillings, or a lovely protein addition to kanji (especially sweetened ragi kanji)!

- *Soaked groundnuts are eaten as a raw side dish at ashram breakfasts. They also make a nice crunchy addition to salads.*
- *Other nuts - such as almonds, walnuts, pecans, cashews, and even pumpkin and sunflower seeds - can be soaked in a similar manner.*

Sprouts —
The Power Food

When one thinks about food sources, and getting the most nutritional bang for your buck, there's nothing more concentrated, more nutritionally potent than nuts, legumes and seeds. After all, they contain everything needed to become a healthy, vibrant plant and to continue their particular species for generations to come.

Though seeds and nuts are packed with vitamins and minerals regardless of preparation, their substantial nutrients are most accessible just as the plant is about to spring forth from the dormant seed. Sprouting, therefore, is a method of coaxing out this vitality and maximizing nutrition.

Virtually any seed, nut, legume or grain can be sprouted, though not all are easily digestible in a raw state. Even if these items are eventually cooked, sprouting ahead of time can dramatically increase the nutritional accessibility of the item as well as reduce the cooking time.

While many sprouts can be eaten raw, there are some varieties (especially the chanas) that need to be blanched / parboiled, because they can be hard to digest. When sprouting any seed, nut or legume, check their edibility. Some sprouts (like those of the nightshade family) are toxic if consumed sprouted.

SPROUTING INSTRUCTIONS

The following instructions for sprouting moong dal can be used to sprout other legumes, though soaking and sprouting time may vary:

1. Measure the amount of moong beans needed for a recipe or meal side (generally 1 cup of dried beans will yield enough sprouts for 6-8 people per meal).
2. Place the dried beans on a stainless plate or other contained surface. Pick through the beans and discard any discoloured ones, or any debris that may have been packed along with the moong.
3. Place the good beans in a stainless steel or glass bowl.
4. Rinse repeatedly with warm or tepid water until the drain-off runs clear.
5. Cover the moong with fresh, tepid / warm water, so that the depth of the water is at least twice the depth of the beans.
6. Cover the bowl with a plate, lid or taut tea towel. Allow to sit for 6-8 hours or overnight.

7. The moong is ready to sprout when the beans plump up (double to triple in size) and the green skins just begin to split. (The small white sprout tails may also be visible at this point.)

8. Drain off the excess soaking liquid.

9. Place the wet beans in a clean tea towel or clean piece of loose-weave woven cloth. Tie up the ends of the fabric into a tight bundle. (Alternatively, the beans can be placed in a fine mesh sieve / colander and covered with a wet tea towel. Just ensure the beans are not too spread out – they need to be in a compact environment in order to sprout.)

10. Place the bundle in a colander, and place the colander in a dark, warm environment such as a cooled oven or pantry closet.

- *Sprouting relies on several important factors: moisture, temperature (warmth) and air circulation – all of which will vary from kitchen to kitchen and from one batch of beans to the next. This means that it may take a few attempts at sprouting to find the right combination:*

  - » *Use warm (but not hot) water for rinsing.*
  - » *Keeping the beans tightly packed will help to retain the heat generated by the sprouting process.*
  - » *Fresh dried beans generally produce a greater number of sprouts (with fewer crunchy 'duds').*
  - » *Sometimes a little air is needed for the sprouts to take off – you may need to experiment with various 'proofing' or sprouting locations.*
  - » *Sprouting times will vary; don't check them too often, but do keep the tea towel damp, whichever method you choose.*
  - » *Sprout tails are a measure of the legume's digestibility. Tails that are too short (under ¼") or too long (beyond ¾") are likely to produce excess gas in the system and are better off cooked than eaten raw.*

11. Allow the beans to sit for approximately eight hours, with as little disturbance as possible.
12. Check the progress of the moong. When the beans produce sprouts approximately ¼-½" in length, the sprouts are done.
13. Rinse the moong and serve immediately.

Jaggery — The Medicinal Sugar

Long before white sugar was bleached, refined and brought to market shelves, tropical populations around the world relied on traditional techniques to extract the natural sweetness from sugar canes, date palms and sugar palm trees. The raw juices and saps were boiled over a low temperature, and the condensed syrup poured into moulds. The resulting solid to semi-solid cakes were known as 'jaggery'.

For centuries Ayurveda has recognized jaggery's ability to cleanse toxins from the body (particularly the respiratory system), stimulate the digestive process and help the body recover from heat and exertion.

Unlike its heavily processed cousins, jaggery retains some of the plant's dietary fibre, trace mineral salts as well as iron from the vessels used in its manufacturing. Its distinct taste – slightly reminiscent of molasses, maple syrup and smoky caramel – adds a unique character.

Although jaggery is a more complex carbohydrate than white sugar, and thus digests more slowly, it is almost pure sucrose, and therefore not recommended for diabetic consumption.

Jaggery can be used in any recipe calling for sugar. Because of its rustic manufacturing process, the following steps are needed prior to adding jaggery to a dish:

1. Remove the jaggery cake from its cellophane or jute wrapping. Take off any visible particles (cane flakes, strings, etc.).
2. Use either a heavy-duty knife or large hand grater to shave off pieces of jaggery / break down the cake / block.
3. When you have reduced a sufficient amount of jaggery, place equal parts jaggery and water into a heavy-bottomed pan or cooking vessel (1 cup jaggery to 1 cup water).
4. Boil the jaggery and water over low heat, being careful not to allow the syrup to boil over. Stir frequently.
5. Skim off any impurities that may rise to the surface.
6. Continue to gently boil until the liquid makes a continual drip off a spoon (single string in candy-making terms). This is the consistency needed to sweeten teas, juices and kanjis.
7. To make a thicker syrup suitable for pancakes or to substitute for honey, boil several more minutes until the liquid makes a double-string drip.
8. The mixture can be boiled longer until it reaches a paste-like consistency, which is needed for making traditional Indian sweets. Stir continuously at this point to prevent scorching.

Honey — Enjoying the Natural Sweetness of Life

In today's media there is much talk of 'super foods', foods with unusually high concentrations of beneficial vitamins, minerals, antioxidants and enzymes that not only adequately nourish the body, but go above and beyond to heal the system, restore balance and even prevent or eradicate disease.

Though the idea of food as medicine might be new to some, the Yogic and Ayurvedic systems have been emphasizing food's therapeutic properties for thousands of years. Many of these natural substances – groundnuts, sprouts, turmeric, papaya, ragi – you have read about in the pages of this cookbook. And yet, of all these highly nutritious body healers, there is perhaps one foodstuff more super than all the rest: honey.

There is a distinct parallel between the chemical compositions of raw honey and human blood / haemoglobin. This, along with honey's inherent anti-bacterial, anti-microbial and antiseptic properties, may account for its dominant role in Ayurvedic medications, topical preparations and wound treatments in many of the world's earliest cultures.

Honey itself is the end result of collected flower nectars, which are then processed by hive or cliff-dwelling honeybees. This honey, when mixed with pollen collected by other bees in the colony, forms a complete food source, nourishing the next generation. Because of its connection to the land and environment, honey can be one of the best means of building one's immunity and acclimatizing to local surroundings.

In cooking, of course, honey is primarily used for its sweetness. Composed of a unique combination of fructose and glucose, honey is often absorbed into the system at a slower rate than white or other processed sugars, and may prove to be the better sweetening option for those with blood-sugar sensitivities.

While honey is clearly of enormous health and dietary benefit, there is one thing to keep in mind: honey should not be heated. Doing so (in the form of cooking, baking, boiling or otherwise heat-processing) destroys many of honey's beneficial properties. Ayurveda also warns that consuming heated honey triggers the formation of *ama*, a toxic substance, which is particularly difficult for the body to purge. You can add honey to dishes (such as teas) at the end, after removing the dish from the heat and allowing it to cool slightly. If your recipe calls for a sweetener to be used at a high temperature, experiment with jaggery instead *(See 'Jaggery - The Medicinal Sugar')*. However, if your dish does not require heating, by all means substitute honey for other sweeteners – not only will it be equally delicious, but you might just experience a boost in health at the same time!

Index

AGATHI LEAVES: Leaves of *Sesbania grandiflora*, also known as Hummingbird tree in English and *agasthi* in Hindi. They are available as *agathi keerai* in Tamil Nadu. They should be consumed cooked. Agathi is cooling for the system, and can also cure mouth and tongue ulcers and digestion-related problems. It is especially good for women to consume agathi as it is high in iron. Various parts of the plant have several beneficial properties, and its significance can be gauged from the fact that it has over thirty-five names in Sanskrit, including *Shivamallika*, *Shivashekhara* and *Shivapriya*.

AMARANTH: Various species of *amaranthus* (or amaranth greens), known as *thandukeerai* in Tamil Nadu and *chaulai saag* in Hindi, are nutritious and consumed in various parts of the world. Amaranth leaves are easy to digest, high in protein, have been found to help with diarrhea conditions and in blood-related problems like anaemia.

The amaranth stem is also used as a vegetable. Amaranth seeds are highly nutritious; they can be cooked as a cereal, ground into flour, popped like popcorn, sprouted or toasted. The seeds can be cooked with other whole grains to serve as a meal's starch component, or, added to stir-fries, soups and stews as a thickening agent.

AMCHUR: Dried mango powder, a spice made by grinding dehydrated, dried, unripe mango. The light brown powder preserves the acidic, tart and spicy flavour of unripe mangoes, while imparting a crisp, sourness to curries and marinades. Amchur can also be used as a substitute for tamarind and lemon / lime wherever a tenderizing or souring element is needed.

APPAM TAWA: Wok-like pan or kadhai for making appams.

ASH GOURD: Also called 'winter melon' or 'wax gourd' or *petha* in Hindi and *pooshinikkai* in Tamil, it has several health benefits. It is a wonderful 'brain tonic;' it is tremendously cooling, and helps in stomach problems like constipation and ulcers. Can be cooked as a vegetable or made into

185

halwa or candied, but it is most nutritional when consumed raw, either in salads or as a refreshing juice. Ash gourd is also highly pranic, one of the reasons why it is hung outside new homes in India.

BANANA FLOWER: Known as *vazhai poo* in Tamil and *kele ka phool* in Hindi, it is also called banana blossom. This purplish-red flower is used as a food item, can be added raw into salads, made into pickle or curry, or cooked into poriyal (cooked vegetable dish). High in antioxidants, it has many medicinal qualities, which help for diabetic conditions, excess menstrual bleeding, lowering sugar levels and also purifying the blood.

BANANA STEM: Banana stem is very fibrous in texture. It is eaten raw in salads or *raitas*, or cooked in soups, poriyals (cooked vegetable dishes), or chutneys. It is good for the stomach, detoxifies the body and is widely used in southern India as a remedy for weight loss.

BISIBELEBHATH POWDER: This mixture of spices is used to make bisibelebhath. It is available as a premade masala in Indian grocery stores.

BOTTLE GOURD: Calabash, also known as *suraikkai* in Tamil and *lauki* in Hindi, is a soft vegetable. Having a smooth, thick skin and a soft interior, bottle gourd is often used as a vegetable side. Fresh lauki juice helps alleviate excessive thirst caused by diarrhoea, over-consumption of fatty or fried foods, and diabetes.

CARDAMOM: Pods, seeds and powder. Known as the 'queen of spices', this fragrant spice originated in India, and is often added to sweet and savoury dishes. Seeds help reduce digestive problems and boost kidney function. They are also said to be effective against halitosis. Whole pods add flavour to dishes. Pods are better for storage than ground powder, since they retain flavour longer and can be ground right before use.

CHAAT MASALA: Particular blend of sweet and sour spices used in Indian chaat or snack foods. Chaat masala usually consists of dried mango powder, cumin seeds, ginger, black salt, coriander, black pepper and chilli pepper and is available pre-made in Indian grocery stores. It makes a spicy accompaniment to fresh-cut fruits and vegetables.

CHANA DAL: Also known as Bengal gram or chickpeas. Chana is a major pulse in India. Highly nutritious and protein-rich. Used whole or split, chana is also ground into high-protein gram flour. One of the earliest-grown legumes, it was probably first cultivated over 11,000 years ago in Turkey. See also KABULI CHANA and KALA CHANA.

CHAPATTIS: Soft, thin disc of dough – usually wheat but also of other grains – rolled out after thorough kneading and some resting, and then dry roasted on a slightly concave iron griddle (tawa).

CHIKOO: Indian fruit also known as sapota. Brownish and small with an unpalatable skin; fresh, ripe chikoos are a good source of minerals like potassium, copper, iron and vitamins, and can be added to ice creams, juices, or fruit salads.

CINNAMON: Bark of a tree, long used in Ayurveda and traditional Chinese medicine due to its medicinal qualities. It has been found to help reduce blood sugar, kill bacteria, reduce inflammation, improve digestion, and lower cholesterol. In fact, just the scent of cinnamon has been found to stimulate brain activity. Cinnamon powder can be added for a savoury and rich taste into just about any hot drink, gravy, fruit salad and sweet.

CLOVE: Flower buds of a tree, this aromatic spice is used in flavouring several dishes. In Ayurveda, clove is used to improve circulation, digestion and metabolism. It has been found to have anti-inflammatory and anti-bacterial properties, and is rich in dietary fibre, vitamins and several minerals. For centuries, it was an important component of the spice trade between India and the rest of the world. Sinbad the Sailor, one of the heroes of Arabian Nights, was said to have traded cloves in India.

COCONUT MILK: Extract taken from fresh coconut gratings with hot water; the first extract gives thick milk, and the second a thin one. Used as a thickening agent; also enhances flavour.

CORIANDER LEAVES: Also known as cilantro. Fragrant leaves often used as a garnish. Can also be made into a delicious chutney as a side dish for snacks or tiffin items.

CORIANDER POWDER: Ground coriander seeds. Pungent aroma. This spice is often added to vegetable and gravy dishes to add flavour and assist in digestion.

CORIANDER SEEDS: The dried fruits of coriander are often referred to as seeds. Used in many Indian dishes to add a spicy tang, they are also an ingredient of masala powder. Often eaten as a snack after roasting.

CUMIN: Also known as jeera in Hindi, these seeds are used in Indian seasoning or as a flavouring agent to rice dishes. Can also be ground into a powder which constitutes one of the ingredients of masala powder. Can be boiled along with drinking water to improve digestion.

DHULI DAL: Any dal with the skin removed. See CHANA DAL, MOONG DAL, TOOVAR DAL, URAD DAL.

DOSA FLOUR: Flour made out of a mixture of a grain such as rice, ragi or wheat, and black gram (urad dal), and sold ready-made in some Indian grocery stores. It is an alternative to the traditional batter made at home by soaking and grinding the ingredients.

Dosa is a favourite breakfast in many Indian homes. Its exact place of origin in southern India is unknown, but it was already referred to as a popular dish in Tamil literature 2,000 years ago.

DRUMSTICK: Called *sahjan* or *munga* in Hindi. Comes from the *moringa* tree, sometimes referred to as the 'miracle tree', of which every part has medicinal properties. The long, whip-like pods with soft inner seeds are cooked when tender. They are used in dishes such as *bhaja* in Bengal and sambar and aviyal in southern India. The outer skin is tough and fibrous and should be discarded; only the remaining pulpy flesh and seeds are edible.

Drumstick is highly nutritious and a wonderful source of protein and iron. Regular consumption of drumstick has several benefits. It strengthens the bones, purifies the blood (helps in anaemic conditions), and can help in respiratory conditions. It is advisable for pregnant women to eat drumstick.

DRUMSTICK LEAVES: The leaves of the moringa tree are highly nutritious, being a significant source of beta-carotene, vitamin A, B and C, protein, iron and potassium. The leaves are cooked and used like – or as a substitute for – spinach. They are also commonly dried and crushed into a powder, and used in soups and sauces.

ELEPHANT YAM: A species native to sub-tropical and tropical East Asia, this starchy and high-in-fibre plant-tuber is known as *chenaikizhangu* in Tamil, and *suran* in Hindi. The corm or bulb of this herbaceous plant is referred to as elephant yam. Elephant yam can be baked, fried, stewed or used in place of other tubers in similar preparations. It is particularly cleansing and strengthening for the gastric system and is also used in the treatment of rheumatism. It finds a place as a remedy in the Ayurveda, Siddha and Unani medicinal systems.

Elephant yams can be grown quite easily at home. Neighbours might object though. The plant's flower is called stinky lily because in full bloom, it smells like rotting flesh to attract its pollinators – carrion flies and beetles. The elephant yam is a close relative of the titan arum, which produces the single largest (and some say stinkiest) flower in the natural world.

FENNEL SEEDS: Called *saunf* in India, fennel seeds are commonly eaten after meals for their digestive (particularly gas-relieving) properties. Fennel (in both its whole-seed and powdered forms) is used to flavour food. A relative of the cumin and anise family, fennel imparts an astringent, slightly licorice quality to recipes. It can be used both in its whole-seed (especially in seasonings) and powdered forms.

FENUGREEK SEEDS: Also called *methi dana*, they are a commonly used spice in Indian cooking. The leaves of the fenugreek plant are used too, either fresh or dried, and make a nice addition to *parathas*, rotis and dal. Fenugreek seeds are used as the bitter component in various spice mixtures, such as the Bengali mixed spice, panch phoron, and southern Indian sambar powder. In the Ayurvedic tradition, the seeds are noted to contain bitter substances considered to be anti-diabetic as well as cooling to the body's system.

FLAXSEED: Also known as *alsi* or *teesi* in Hindi and *ali vidai* in Tamil, this high-fibre seed comes in both brown, yellow or gold colour. It is often made into oil and also sprouted, roasted or powdered for use in various dishes.

GARAM MASALA POWDER: Garam masala is a commonly found spice preparation in many Indian kitchens. Typically made of a blend of cumin, cardamom, black pepper, cinnamon, and clove, it imparts spiciness and pungency to dishes without the use of chilli. The exact proportions of garam masala spices vary from region to region, and kitchen to kitchen, but pre-made blends are also available in mass markets and grocery stores.

GHEE: Ghee is made by first making butter, and then removing the milk solids, and thus clarifying it. Ghee is known to stimulate the digestive process and is also a frequent base for Ayurvedic medicines.

GINGELLY OIL: Sesame oil (also known as til oil) is an edible vegetable oil derived from sesame seeds. Besides being used as cooking oil in southern India, it is often used as a flavour enhancer in Chinese, Japanese, Korean and to a lesser extent in Southeast Asian cuisine, where the seeds are usually roasted before the oil is extracted. The oil from the nutrient-rich seed is popular in alternative medicine, traditional massages and treatments.

GRAM FLOUR: Gram flour is a flour made from ground chana (Bengal gram or chickpeas). Also referred to as *besan* and chickpea flour. Gram flour contains a high proportion of carbohydrates and protein, but no gluten.

HIBISCUS: Also known as 'rose mallow' and 'Jamaica' flower, hibiscus has long been used in Ayurvedic and Chinese medicine. High in anti-oxidants, it has also been found to help with high blood pressure, high cholesterol, diabetes and heart-related ailments. It is very cooling for the system, and is used in face packs for acne and hair treatments for dandruff and dry scalp. Pregnant and nursing women, however, should avoid hibiscus. Those on any kind of medication should also consult a physician before consuming hibiscus. Hibiscus can be made into syrup or sauce, added to salads or blended into juice or teas.

IDIYAPPAM: String hoppers – a steamed rice-flour noodle / patty made of flour, a dough pressed into noodle form, extruded through a sieve or press and cooked either in banana leaf or an idli steamer. Idiyappam is popular in southern India and some parts of Sri Lanka and typically served either with curry or chutney.

IDLI: A fluffy, cake-like savoury of a flattened-bun shape. The flour is made out of a mixture of a grain such as rice, ragi or wheat, and black gram (urad dal). Idli preparation has undergone some amount of change in the last millennium. Its ingredients, as listed in the oldest known Kannada-language encyclopedia in 1025 AD, include buttermilk, curds, cumin, coriander, pepper and asafoetida, besides urad dal.

JACKFRUIT: A fast-growing tropical Asian tree *(Artocarpus heterophyllus)* of the mulberry family. The very large edible fruit of this tree has a characteristic smell, and – when raw – its taste is vaguely reminiscent of vanilla and pineapple. The young fruit can also be prepared as a vegetable, while the seeds (when pressure cooked) add a delightful hearty texture to sambars and curries. Jackfruit has been found to have anti-ageing, antioxidant and anti-ulcer properties.

JAGGERY: Two different types, made from the products of sugarcane and the palm tree. Jaggery has been produced in India for many millennia. One of the first people to document its production was Nearchos, a general in Alexander's army, who, during his travels in the Indus Valley, described a reed which produced honey without bees!

Jaggery is highly pranic, and is a healthier alternative to white sugar. It is known as 'the medicinal sugar' in Ayurveda. Eating jaggery is also very useful in health problems like dry cough, cough with sputum, indigestion and constipation.

Sometimes, a chemical called 'superphosphate' is added to make the jaggery look light in colour. It is best to have the other kind, which is usually dark and rough looking.

JOWAR: A cereal, called sorghum in English and cholam in Tamil. A hardy crop, it gives the highest yield for effort invested during cultivation. Consumed as porridge, malts, breads or popped like corn. Preliminary research has shown that jowar may protect against diabetes, cancer and high cholesterol.

KABULI CHANA: White chana dal or white chickpeas or garbanzo beans. They are hard, knobby, beige beans about $^3/_8$" round. Its nutty and creamy flavour, firm texture and minimal fat content make it a versatile ingredient. It is used in several popular Indian dishes like chana masala, chole palak and various chaats, as well as in many Middle Eastern recipes like hummus and falafel. It can also be added to soups and salads. See also CHANA DAL.

KALA CHANA: Black Bengal gram or black chickpeas. Dhuli chana dal (split Bengal gram) is produced by removing the outer layer of the kala chana and then splitting the kernel. See also CHANA DAL.

KAMBU: The Tamil word for pearl millet, also called *bajra* in Hindi. A source of many vitamins, minerals, protein and starch, kambu is known to be beneficial to the digestive, nervous and circulatory system. Several dishes using kambu are common in India, including rotis and dosas.

KAVUNI ARISI: Also known as 'black rice'. This whole grain is native to Asia, and has been recently recognized for its abundant health and nutritional benefits. It was also known as 'forbidden rice' in China, because only royalty were allowed to eat it. High in antioxidants, black rice is a more wholesome alternative to white rice, and can be used in any recipe as a substitute for white rice. Its nutty taste gives a tasty addition to sweets and salads.

LEMONGRASS: Used for hundreds of years in ancient medicines thanks to its innumerable health benefits. Recent studies indicate lemongrass can help in preventing cancer. It is also known as 'fever grass' for its support during periods of fever or illness. A wonderful detoxifying agent for the body, it is also good for the digestive system and for women having menstruation pains.

MAIDA: Refined wheat flour. When feasible, a healthier alternative is whole wheat flour.

MOAR MOLAGA: Chillies that have been soaked in salted buttermilk and then dried. These are deep-fried in oil and used as accompaniment to curd rice, etc. They are used instead of pickle in a typical Tamil Nadu meal.

MOONG DAL: Green gram or *mung* bean, also called *payatham paruppu* in Tamil. A source of protein and iron, it helps control blood pressure and keep cancer at bay.

NANNARI ROOT: Also known as *anantmul* in Hindi, meaning 'endless root', a reference to its long root system. Nannari root is a highly valued tonic in Ayurveda. Brewed into a hot beverage, or blended with jaggery into a syrup, nannari is known for its pain relieving, inflammation reducing and cooling properties. Nannari root can also be boiled along with drinking water.

NIGELLA SEEDS: Called *kalonji* in Hindi and *karun jeeragam* in Tamil. A spice used in Indian cuisine to flavour curry, vegetables and pulses.

OKRA: Also known as lady's finger in English, *bhindi* in Hindi, and *vendakkai* in Tamil. It is valued for its edible green seed-pods, which are high in fibre and vitamin C. Its seeds, when cooked, produce a natural thickening agent.

PANCH PHORON: A whole spice blend consisting of five spices – fennel, black mustard, nigella, cumin and fenugreek seeds. Part of the cuisine in eastern India, Nepal and Bangladesh, is consumed with vegetables and lentils, and in pickles.

PANEER: Paneer or cottage cheese is an integral part of South Asian cooking. Paneer is a versatile dairy product, used in desserts, snacks and main courses. Made without rennet, paneer is a vegetarian-friendly protein source.

PAPAYA: This is one of the most nutritious fruits. Among various other benefits, it cleanses the system and is very healing for people with ulcers or stomach / digestive problems.

PARBOILED RICE: Rice that has been soaked, steamed and dried after harvesting, making it easier to remove the bran. The parboiling process forces nutrients from the husk into the grain itself, making parboiled rice closer in nutritional value to brown rice than processed white rice.

PLANTAINS: Starchy bananas, used as a staple food source throughout the tropics. While sweet bananas are typically eaten raw, plantains are generally peeled and cooked in much the same way potatoes are, i.e. boiled, fried, steamed and mashed.

PUMPKIN SEEDS: Pumpkin seeds are subtly sweet and nutty with a chewy texture. Usually encased in a yellow-white husk, although some varieties of pumpkins produce seeds without shells. Pumpkin seeds can be toasted or eaten raw, can be ground and used as a base for dips and chutneys, or added to salads for a crunchy taste. They are a good source of insoluble fibre (which aids digestion), protein and minerals.

PUTTU: A southern Indian and Sri Lankan breakfast dish which is powdery in texture, and can be served with any gravy or with bananas. Another variety of puttu is made of steamed cylinders of ground rice layered with coconut. This is popular in the Indian state of Kerala.

RAGI: A fast-growing cereal plant cultivated in warm countries and regions with poor soils. Referred to as a 'super cereal' by many nutrition scientists, it is high in calcium and protein and has shown anti-diabetic, anti-cancer and anti-ageing potential. Part of the Indian diet for 4,000 years, ragi is prepared as *laddus*, cookies, dosas, pakodas and many other dishes. Unfortunately, ragi cultivation is on the decline in India, having dropped 95 per cent in the last two decades.

RAJMA: Red kidney beans. Part of the regular diet in northern India, it is often prepared with gravy as a vegetable side.

RIDGE GOURD: Commonly known as *turai* or *turiya* in Hindi and *peerkangai* in Tamil, it is an extremely popular vegetable in African, Asian and Arabic countries. It is also known by other names such as *loofah, luffa, tori,* etc. It is a dark green, ridged vegetable with white seeds embedded in white spongy flesh. All species of ridge gourd are edible, but must be consumed before they mature, or they turn too woody and fibrous to eat. Ridge gourd is loaded with nutrients such as dietary fibre, vitamin C, riboflavin, zinc, thiamin, iron and magnesium. It is also low in fat and calories.

ROSE PETAL: Consumption of rose petals (in tea, oil, or as rosewater) helps with sore throats, digestive problems, urinary problems and painful menstruations. It is also used for treating wounds and inflammation, acne, and for cosmetic purposes. Rose petals are used in salads, jams, sweets, syrups, candy and drinks.

SAGO: A starch derived from the stem of sago palm. Called *sabu dana* in Hindi or *javvarisi* in Tamil, sago is a common breakfast dish in Maharashtra and is very easy to prepare. It is used to make *payasams*, beverages and crispy *vadas*. It is often consumed during fasting periods.

SAMBAR: A dal and vegetable-based soup that is a typical part of the southern Indian meal. A mixture of several vegetables and spices, the word sambar likely derives from an old Tamil word *champaaram*, meaning spicy condiments.

SAMBAR POWDER: This cumin, coriander and chilli-based spice mix is typically used in southern Indian homes on a daily basis. It is the main flavouring agent for sambar. Though it is readily available in shops, it can also be made at home.

SANJEEVINI: Sanjeevini is a nutritious flour available at the Isha Yoga Centre. This 100 per cent natural-flour product contains fourteen important ingredients (including whole grains, pulses and nut-meats), which provide energy and balanced nutrition. It is available for delivery throughout India, and can be ordered at ishashoppe.com.

SNAKE GOURD: Also known as 'Chinese cucumber', this vegetable in the form of a long, green pod can grow to well over a metre in length. Snake gourd cools the system and its roots and leaves are highly medicinal. The juice of snake gourd leaves is often consumed for common ailments. Snake gourd is used in sambars, dry curries or fried with stuffing. Snake gourd can also be peeled and eaten raw, and is easily used in place of cucumbers in salads.

SOOJI: Also known as rava (semolina), it is the coarsely ground endosperm of a type of wheat called durum wheat. It can be used to make puddings, sweets (halwa), uppuma, breakfast cereals, and even added to bread flour. As an alternative to cornmeal, sooji can be used to flour the baking surface to prevent sticking. In bread-making, a small proportion of sooji added to the usual mix of flour produces a hearty, European-style crust.

STAR ANISE: Star-shaped, dark-brown pod that contains a seed in each of its arms. Coming from an evergreen tree native to China, it is used to give a licorice flavour to savoury dishes.

TAMARIND: Known as *imli* in Hindi and *puli* in Tamil, the edible pod-like fruit of the tamarind tree is an integral part of Indian cuisine, imparting its distinctive sweet-sour flavour to dishes. The ripe pods are also favourite snacks for kids, making the tree a target for many well-aimed missiles.

Tamarind is so embedded in southern Indian cuisine that the

Tamil word for a sour taste is *puli*. Tamarind's relationship with the Indian psyche goes deeper than taste buds. Tamarind trees are often integral parts of plotlines in myths and stories, usually as the place where ghosts 'hang out', to descend on unprepared passers-by.

TOOVAR DAL: Pigeon peas. It is most commonly sold and cooked in its split, skinless form. With its skin intact, it is a greenish-brown colour and when skinless, it is yellow. It is especially popular in the West and in southern India. It cooks quickly and does not require to be soaked in advance. This is the main ingredient in traditional sambar.

TULSI LEAVES: A highly revered plant in India, it has tremendous medicinal properties and is used in Ayurveda. Tulsi is rich in antioxidants and is renowned for its restorative powers. It has many known benefits – it is an adaptogen (compounds that improve the body's ability to handle stress) and relieves stress, bolsters immunity, enhances stamina, provides support during the cold season, promotes a healthy metabolism and is believed to contribute to longevity. Traditionally, every Indian household had a tulsi plant in the backyard.

TURMERIC POWDER: Turmeric is a spice that is widely used in Indian cuisine. It is an important ingredient of most commercial curry powders. Turmeric is also used to give a yellow colour to some prepared mustards. It is believed to have originated in South Asia.

Turmeric has been used in Ayurveda, and its medicinal benefits are numerous. For people with excess mucus problems, consuming turmeric takes away the excess phlegm in the tract. It has a healing effect, is very supportive for the digestive system and can kill the cancerous cells in the body.

UPPUMA: A popular Indian breakfast dish, cooked as a porridge from semolina or course rice flour. Its name is a combination of *uppu* and *mavu* which mean salt and flour respectively in most southern Indian languages.

URAD DAL: Black gram. Native to India, it is used extensively in preparations such as dosa and idli. The gram is black when whole, and white when split.

Sadhguru

Yogi, mystic, and visionary, Sadhguru is a spiritual master with a difference. An arresting blend of profundity and pragmatism, his life and work serve as a reminder that Yoga is not an esoteric discipline from an outdated past, but a contemporary science, vitally relevant to our times. Probing, passionate and provocative, insightful, logical and unfailingly witty, Sadhguru's talks have earned him the reputation of a speaker and opinion-maker of international renown.

With speaking engagements that take him around the world, he is widely sought after by prestigious global forums to address issues as diverse as human rights, business values, and social, environmental and existential issues. He has been a delegate to the United Nations Millennium World Peace Summit, is a member of the World Council of Religious and Spiritual Leaders and Alliance for New Humanity, a special invitee to the Australian Leadership Retreat, Tallberg Forum, Indian Economic Summit 2005-2008, as well as a regular speaker at the World Economic Forum in Davos. With a celebratory engagement with life on all levels, Sadhguru's areas of active involvement encompass fields as diverse as architecture and visual design, poetry and painting, ecology and horticulture, sports and music. He is the author and designer of several unique buildings and consecrated spaces at the Isha Yoga Centre, which have received wide attention for their combination of intense sacred power with strikingly innovative eco-friendly aesthetics.

isha.sadhguru.org

Isha Foundation

Isha Foundation is a non-profit human-service organization supported by over three million volunteers in over 200 centres worldwide. Recognizing the possibility of each person to empower another, Isha Foundation has created a massive movement that is dedicated to addressing all aspects of human well-being without ascribing to any particular ideology, religion or race. From its powerful Yoga programmes to its inspiring projects for society and environment, Isha's activities are designed to create an inclusive culture that is the basis for global harmony and progress.

Isha Foundation is also involved in several path-breaking outreach initiatives: Action for Rural Rejuvenation (ARR) enhances the quality of rural life through health care and disease prevention, community revitalization, women empowerment, the creation of sustainable livelihoods and Yoga programmes. Isha Vidhya empowers rural children with quality education. Project GreenHands (PGH) initiates mass tree planting and creates a culture of care for the environment to keep this planet liveable for future generations.

Isha's unique approach to cultivating human potential has gained worldwide recognition and reflects in Isha Foundation's special consultative status with the Economic and Social Council (ECOSOC) of the United Nations.

isha.sadhguru.org